STUDENT'S SOLUTIONS MANUAL

to accompany

MATHEMATICS FOR ELEMENTARY SCHOOL TEACHERS

STUDENT'S SOLUTIONS MANUAL

TIM MOGILL

to accompany

MATHEMATICS FOR ELEMENTARY SCHOOL TEACHERS

O'DAFFER • CHARLES • COONEY
DOSSEY • SCHIELACK

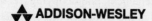 ADDISON-WESLEY

An imprint of Addison Wesley Longman, Inc.

Reading, Massachusetts • Menlo Park, California • New York • Harlow, England
Don Mills, Ontario • Sydney • Mexico City • Madrid • Amsterdam

Reproduced by Addison-Wesley Publishing Company Inc. from camera-ready copy supplied by the author.

ISBN   0-201-59135-9

1 2 3 4 5 6 7 8 9 10 VG 00999897

CONTENTS

Student's Solutions Manual

to accompany

Mathematics for Elementary School Teachers

SECTION 1.1

1. Responses will vary among students.

3. Responses will vary among students.

5. Responses will vary among students. Recall that the manufacturer did remove that particular doll from the market. The outcry was caused by a perceived gender bias.

7. Responses will vary among students. Some may produce a technical definition similar to: the shape is a closed planar figure formed by three segments each of which intersects two others only at endpoints. Others may use more generic terms such as: the figure is unbroken with three corners and straight sides.

9. Responses will vary among students. Some may chose to use the symbols for computations, others symbols for numbers such as π or e. Some may use more esoteric symbols that they have encountered such as $\sum$.

11. a. Responses will vary among students. The message conveyed by the graph is ambiguous. Although better than 1 in 10 women do not conduct self-exams, over half (38% + 4% + 11%) do follow the once per month recommendation. Are we pleased that over half of the women do work for early detection and thus enhance survival chances or are we displeased that a significant proportion do not follow the recommendation?

    b. **One self-exam per month** is the most frequent occurrence, performed by 38% of the women responding to the survey.

    c. **Fifty three percent** (38% + 4% + 11%) of the women responding to the survey perform self-exams at least once a month.

13. A **fraction** calculator would be used. A four-function calculator with key-strokes 3÷8+4÷5= would give a decimal result.

15. A **graphing calculator** would serve the purpose.

17. The selection will vary among students. In their responses the students should, perhaps, include the idea that the choice of presentation is related not only to what is being presented but also is dependent upon the characteristics of the audience.   To many, the equation may be meaningless. The tabular presentation is the most obvious.

19. The responses will vary among students. Some possible considerations are: the extent to which each is considered to be open to interpretation, the degrees to which 'new ground' can be broken in each area, the extent of relation to reality, the part played by creativity.

21. a. The solution requires that the spreadsheet be continued until the value of the car is less than $8000. Each entry in the B column after year 1 is .8 of the value immediately above. So: A3 = 1, B3 = .8 * B2 = 16,000;   A4 = 2, B4 = .8 * B3 = 12,800; A5 = 3, B5 = 10,240; A6 = 4, B6 = 8,192; A7 =- 5, B7 = 6,553.60.

    b. The value is less than $8,000 in **year 5** and the spreadsheet has **7 rows**.

23.

Number of hours	cost: plan A	cost: plan B
5	90	140
6	108	148
7	126	156
8	144	164
9	162	172
10	**180**	**180**
11	198	188

The plans are equal in cost for ten hours of play. Plan B is more economical for **11 or more hours** of play.

25. Responses will vary among students.

27.

Hens	Rabbits	Feet
50	0	50
40	10	120
30	**20**	140

Thus the farmer has **30 hens and 20 rabbits**. Note that in employing a spreadsheet it is often useful to begin with rather coarse increments to establish the range containing the required value. One may then use smaller increments. In this case the broader increment contained the exact answer.

SECTION 1.2

1. The four examples show that adding 0 to a number results in the number. One might generalize from these examples that the sum of 0 and any number is the original number.

3. a. An **arithmetic sequence** has consecutive terms with a common difference.
    b. Consecutive terms of a **geometric sequence** have a common ratio.

5. Responses will vary. Possibilities include any number ending in 1 or 9 as a counterexample. For example, 11 squared is 121, a number that doesn't end in 4, 5, 6, or 9.

7. a. Hypothesis: an odd number is added to an even number; conclusion: the sum is an odd number.
    b. Hypothesis: a figure has four connected sides; conclusion: it is a quadrilateral.
    c. Hypothesis: it rains on Tuesday; conclusion: it will be nice on Wednesday.
    d. Hypothesis: the square of a number is even; conclusion: the number is even.

9. A statement of the form 'If p, then q.' is called a conditional or an *implication*. Logically, an implication is true in all cases except that in which the hypothesis is true and the conclusion is false. Jack's statement "If the temperature is below 50°, then I won't play tennis." is an implication.
    a. Because the general conditions of both hypothesis and conclusion of Jack's original conditional are supported in this particular situation, this case indicates Jack **told the truth** in his original conditional statement.
    b   Because the hypothesis, but not the conclusion, is supported, this case indicates Jack **did not tell the truth** in his original statement.
    c. This specific case does not meet the conditions set forth in the hypothesis of Jack's general conditional. But **Jack's implication is true, and he did not lie.**
    d. This case is the same as c.

11. a. This is an example of **proportional** reasoning (7/10 = 28/40).
   b. The conclusion that an even number ends in 0, 2, 4, 6, or 8 was most probably reached by **inductive** reasoning. The statement could, however, be a definition.
   c. This is an example of **invalid deductive reasoning**. The accepted conditional is 'All triangles have three sides.' (If a geometric figure is a triangle, then that figure has three sides.) The particular condition is 'ABC is a triangle,' which affirms the hypothesis. But the conclusion of the conditional is not correctly applied to the specific instance.
   d. This is an example of **inductive** reasoning.

13. a. This is a **valid** example of deductive reasoning by affirming the hypothesis.
   b. This reasoning is **invalid**. It is an example of **assuming the converse**.
   c. This example is also **invalid**. It is an example of the fallacy of **assuming the inverse**.
   d. **Invalid**, this is another example of **assuming the converse**.

15. The examples suggest that the product 1..11 x 12 will be of the form 13...32 with the number of threes one less than the number of ones. Thus 111111 x 12 = **1333332**. A calculator check shows this to be correct.

17. Jennifer employed inductive reasoning. Indeed, the numbers 4, 24, 44, and 64 all end in 4 and are evenly divisible by four. Since each of these numbers end in 4, Jennifer generalized that all numbers ending in 4 are evenly divisible by 4. Jennifer's **generalization is false**. The number 14 serves as a counterexample.

19. Responses will vary. Possibilities include: The keystrokes 6, +, 3, =, =, =, = produce the numbers 9, 12, 15, 18. These form an arithmetic sequence. The keystrokes 6, x, 2, = ,=, =, = produce 12, 72, 432, 2592. These form a geometric sequence.

21. The completed figure is a solid block 5 blocks by 4 blocks by 2 blocks, a total of 40 building blocks. The partial figure has 10 building blocks. Therefore **30 more** building blocks are required.

23. **Both generalizations follow** from the examples given. However, **b is** shown to be **incorrect** with the counterexample 5^2 - 1. Now, for the generalization that the square of an odd number -1 is divisible by 8, consider the following argument: let O be the odd number. Then O = E + 1, E an even number. And O^2 - 1 = $(E + 1)^2$ - 1 = $E^2 + 2E$. Now, an even number has a factor of 2 so let E = 2X. Thus $E^2 + 2E$ = (2X)(2X) + 2(2X) = 4X(X) + 4X = 4X(X + 1). Now, if X is even we have X = 2Y and 4X(X + 1) = 8Y(X+ 1), an expression evenly divisible by 8. If X is odd, then X + 1 is even and a similar argument shows that 4X(X + 1) is divisible b 8. So **a is true** and no counterexample will be found by the students.

25. If two consecutive terms of a geometric sequence are 8 and 12, then r = 12/8 = 1.5 and each term can be calculated from the preceding term by multiplying by 1.5. So the sequence containing 8 and 12 would continue 18, 27, ... **Kevin is correct**.

27. Responses will vary among students. Some responses might include: If a person works for Sleezy, then that person will make a fortune; If you work hard, then you will get promoted fast; If you are trained by Sleezy, then you will be smart.

29. Responses will vary. They may include the ideas: The ad promotes the following conditionals: 'If you want to feel your best, then take one Vigorous Vitamin each day' and 'If a person takes Vigorous Vitamins, then that person cares about their health'. Frieda mistakenly has assumed the converse of the first ad statement and has assumed the inverse of the second ad statement. Although Frieda has misinterpreted the ad, she has most probably reached the conclusions hoped for by the ad maker.

31. Bridget will weigh 140 - 3 - 8(1.5) lbs = **125 lbs**.

33. Responses will vary among students. An argument might be something like: The bugs are assuming the conditional that if a person or animal slides down the slide, then that person or animal will become ensnared in the web. Some small animal does slide down. Thus the animal is ensnared. The bugs did pull it off. The final conclusion is that the bugs will eat like kings.

35. First, use the complete diagonal to get the magic number of 34. Now, column 3 is missing one number which must make the sum of that column 34. The number is 11. Continuing in the same manner we find that row 2 is missing a 5, column 1 must have a 9, the second diagonal needs a 6. Now put a 12 in the column 4 blank and 15 in the row 4 blank. Complete the perfect square by placing a 3 in row 1. Now all rows, columns, and diagonals add to 34.

16	3	2	13
5	10	11	8
9	6	7	12
4	15	14	1

SECTION 1.3

1. Responses will vary among students. Can you do this mentally? With paper/pencil? Need a calculator?

3. a. The diagram shows that the numbers of boxes in consecutive rows form an arithmetic sequence beginning with 1 and with a common difference of 1. One could extend the sequence, adding all the terms, until the sum is 21. $1 + 2 + 3 = 6$. $1 + 2 + 3 + 4 = 10$. $1 + 2 + 3 + 4 + 5 = 15$. $1 + 2 + 3 + 4 + 5 + 6 = 21$. Thus there are **6** boxes in the bottom row.

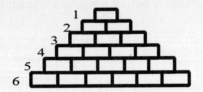

   b. The diagram shows that when the sixth row is drawn, the number of boxes totals to 21 and the last row contains 6 boxes.

5. This problem has **one solution: 2 quarters, 2 dimes, and 1 nickel**. One might argue: since there must be 5 coins, none larger than a quarter, there must be at least 2 quarters because no combination of 4 or 5 nickels and dimes total to 75 cents. There cannot be 3 quarters because the total would be attained in 3 coins. So there must be 2 quarters. The remaining 3 coins must total 25 cents and this can be done in only one way: 2 dimes and 1 nickel.

7. The responses will vary among students. Possibilities include: Represent the situation with an equation and solve the equation (problem f); draw a diagram (problem b); make a table (problems a and c); use a list making approach (problem d); use reasoning to match and eliminate possible matches (problem e).

9. Responses will vary among students. Among the considerations are: type of phone, auxiliary equipment, basic time package, time spent in roaming areas.

11. One might use reasoning and table-making. For example: let one number be XY and the other YX and that XY + YX = 77 and XY - YX = 27. Assume that when the units are added there is no carry into the tens column.

X	Y	XY	YX	SUM	DIFFERENCE
0	7	7	70	77	-63
1	6	16	61	77	-45
2	5	25	52	77	-27
3	4	34	43	77	-9
4	3	43	34	77	9
5	2	52	25	77	27

Thus we see that the two numbers are **52 and 25.**

13. Responses will vary. The problem could be approached with the guess-check-revise strategy:
   a. Suppose you had 1 half dollar and 1 quarter. Then your remaining coins must be dimes, nickels, or pennies because another half dollar or quarter would give change for a dollar. Now, you could have up to 4 dimes and 4 pennies without change for a dollar. So the total is **$1.19**.
   b. Suppose you had a quarter. Then you could also have 4 dimes and 4 pennies and not be able to give change for a half dollar. So you could have **69 cents**. You could also have any number of half dollars.
   c. You could have 4 nickels and 4 pennies: **24 cents**. You could also have any number of dimes, quarters, or half dollars in any combination.
   d. You could have a nickel and 4 pennies, **9 cents** and any number of dimes, quarters, or half dollars.
   e. You could have 4 pennies, **4 cents**, or any number of nickels, dimes, quarters, or half dollars in any combination.

15. Responses will vary. One might reason this way: The most efficient way to cut grass is to pass over each section of grass only once. So imagine that for each pattern the grass is cut into rectangular strips 30" wide laid end to end. The cutter would have to walk the total length of the strips. But since the area of the lawn is the same for either pattern, the total length is also the same. Thus the distance walked is the same. Any difference would be in the mechanics of turning.

17. Responses will vary among students. Most frequently used would probably be guess-check-revise.

19. Responses will vary among groups of students.

21. Responses will vary among students.

23. Responses will vary among students. One solution is: Let S = single deliveries, T = twins, R = triplets. Then S + T + R = 40 and T + R = 8. So S = 32 leaving 21 children born in multiple deliveries. So 2T + 3R = 21 and since T + R = 8, we have 2 (8 - R) + 3 R = 21. So R = 5 and T = 3. **There were 32 single babies, 3 sets of twins, and 5 collections of triplets**.

25. Response will vary among students. If B = slices eaten by Brenda, then 2B = slices eaten by Tina and 6B (3 times 2B) represents slices eaten by Gene.

27. Responses will vary among pairs of students. One might reason a solution as follows. If the height reached on a particular day is greater or equal to 10' above the bottom, then the beetle will escape on that day. The starting position for each day is 1 ft higher than the day before. So, calling the bottom 10' and the top 0' make a table as:

Day	Start	Max	End
1	10	5	9
2	9	4	8
3	8	3	7
4	7	2	6
5	6	1	5
6	5	0	ESCAPE!!!

29. Responses will vary among students. 'Orientation to the problem' is similar to 'Understand in the problem', 'Produce relevant ideas and form and test hypotheses for solving the problem' is similar to 'Develop a plan". The strategies are similar.

SECTION 1.4

1. 1/2, .5, and 50 % are different representations of the same number.

3. Responses will vary among students. Different representation are appropriate for different situations. The fraction representation is more appropriate for: "I lost half my marbles." than is the decimal or percent representation because marbles are a set of discrete objects.

5. Answers will vary among students. Some students may recognize that the expressions for area bring apparently disparate figures under a common umbrella. The ability to generalize is one of the great strengths of mathematics.

7. Responses will vary among students. A possibility is to center the circle at the intersection of the diagonals of the square.

9. Answers will vary among students. One model would be to represent the players by the vertices of a rectangle and the matches by the sides and diagonals of the rectangle. Another model would be to represent the players as 4 points on a circle and the matches by all chords joining these 4 points.

11. Responses will vary among students. The text has implied that mathematics involves some algorithmic executions, some abstract concepts, conjecture by induction and proof by deduction, real world problem solving, and computation and investigation with the aid of technology. All of these should receive adequate attention in mathematics classes.

13. Responses will vary among students. One possibility is the top view of a rectangular solid with a cylindrical hole through it.

15. Responses will vary among students. Mathematics includes mental operations, paper/pencil operations, and operations executed with the aid of technology.

17. Responses will vary among students. One possibility is: If A jogs 10 miles at a rate of 8 minutes per mile, how long does it take her to jog the 10 miles? A related problem with the same numbers and operations is: In a corn shucking contest B shucks 10 ears per minute. How many ears can he shuck in 8 minutes?

19. If 3" is used to represent 10', the paper would have to be 9" by 12" to contain a scaled representation of a 30' by 40' plan. Since the paper is only 8 ½ by 11 inches and we are restricted to whole numbers, the next largest scale would be **2" represents 10'**. The house plan would occupy a 6" by 8" area of the paper.

21. Responses will vary among students.

23. Applying the same method we multiply 3 and 2, writing the 6. We then multiply 3 and 3, then 4 and 2 adding the sums, getting 17, write the 7 and remember the 1. Finally we multiply 4 and 3, getting 12, and add the remembered 1 getting 13. So the product is **1376**.

CHAPTER 1 REVIEW EXERCISES

1. Answers will vary among students.

3. Responses will vary. Possibilities include:
   a. A counterexample is $10 \div 1 = 10$.
   f. A rectangle may have sides that are not equal, say 3 and 4. Thus it is not a square.
   c. Consider the product of 7 and 2. The product is 14, an even number.

5. a. The conclusion, obtained by **affirming the hypothesis,** is that angle C of figure ABCD is a right angle.
   b. The conclusion, Alice's coffee was not heated in a microwave for 100 seconds, is obtained by **denying the conclusion.**

7. Using **proportional reasoning** to solve the problem, we have 3 is to 2 as 750 is to 500. So Debra received 750 shares.

9. a and b. i.   22, 33, 44, 55, 66, 77, 88, 99, <u>110</u>, <u>121</u>, <u>132</u>:   **arithmetic, d = 11.**
            ii. 1, 11, 12, 22, 23, 33, 34, 44, <u>45</u>, <u>55</u>, <u>56</u>: **neither**, sequence is formed by alternately adding 10 and 1
            iii. 2, 6, 18, 54, 162, 486, 1458, <u>4374</u>, <u>13,122</u>, <u>39,366</u>: **geometric, r = 3.**

11. a. The first column is an arithmetic sequence with d = 1. The second column is an arithmetic sequence with d = 2. Continuing these sequences we get the next three rows as: **7 13;   8 15;   and 9 17.**
    b. We also note that the entries in the second column are 1 less than twice the corresponding first column entries. So the 25th row would be **25   49.**

13. Responses will vary. A possibility is:
    a. Use a guess-check-revise strategy.
    b. Ball - $35, shoes - $50: total $85 is high. So revise the ball down. Ball - $34, shoes - $49. Total $83. So the ball did cost **$34 and the shoes cost $49.**

15. These two problems are essentially the same because they can be represented by a common geometric model. The vertexes in the model can represent either the people or the desks, the segments can represent the cables or a pairing of riders.

A   B

D   C

17. Responses will vary among students. A possibility is: The graph could have been produced by GM to show that if families have one car, to insure reliability more families purchase GM car that any other.

19. a. The common aspect of the figures is that the circle must be inside the square. The orientations of the square with respect to the circle may differ.

    b. Responses will vary. A set of possibilities is:

        i   ii   iii

21. Fill in the following table:

Number of Items	Cost Up Front Plan	Straight $40 Cost
0	100	0
1	120	40
2	140	80
3	160	120
4	180	160
5	200	200

The breakeven point is **5 items purchased**.

23. Answers will vary among groups. Problem-solving skills refer to the ability of individuals or groups of persons to implement the problem-solving process with the end result of arriving at suitable strategies to solve particular problems.

25. Caitlin is correct. She could pass the same person more than once and someone she passed could repass her to finish ahead of her.

SECTION 2.1

1. Equivalent sets are sets that have the same number of elements. Let set A = {@, #, $} and set B = {%, ^, &}. Because we can establish the one-to-one correspondence: @ and %, # and ^,and $ and &, the sets A and B are equivalent.

3. Let set S = {a,b,c,d,e,f,g,h,i,j}. The only subset of S, or of any set for that matter, that illustrates the number 0 is the null or empty set, { }. Some subsets of S illustrating the number 1 are {a}, {b}, {c}; the number 2: {a,b}, {a,c}, {b,c}; 3: {a,b,c}, {a,b,d}, {b,c,d}; 4: {a,b,c,d}, {a,c,d,e}, {a,d,e,f}; 5: {a,,b,c,d,e}, {a,c,d,e,f}, {b,c,d,e,f,}; 6: {a,b,c,d,e,f}, {b,c,d,e,f,g}, {c,d,e,f,g,h}; 7: {a,b,c,d,e,f,g}, {b,d,e,f,g,h,i}, {c,d,e,f,g,h,i}; 8: {a,b,c,d,e,f,g,h}, {b,c,d,e,f,g,h,i}, {c,d,e,f,g,h,i,j}; 9: {a,b,c,d,e,f,g,h,i}, {a,b,c,d,e,f,g,h,j}, {a,c,d,e,f,g,h,i,j}; and finally, only one set, S itself, represents the number 10.

5. a. The set Z = {z} is a subset of the set S = {w,x,y,z} because all of the elements of Z are contained in S.
   b. The set A = {a} is not a subset of S because there is at least one element of A that is not in S.

7. a. By definition a set A is a subset of another set B if there are no elements in A that are not in B. S = {w,x,y,z} is a subset of itself because there is no element of S that is not an element of S. This fulfills the conditions of the definition of subset.
   b. The argument may be applied to any set S. This situation is the reason we distinguish between subsets ($\subseteq$) of a set and those subsets that are proper subsets ($\subset$) of a set.

9. a. Consider the set, S, of those whole number that are less than or equal to 5: S = {0,1,2,3,4,5}. This is a finite subset of the whole numbers and it does have a greatest element, 5.
   b Consider the set, T, of whole numbers greater than 5: T = {6,7,8,9,...}. This subset of the whole numbers does not have a greatest element.
   c. There is no infinite subset of the whole numbers that has a greatest element. Consider the following argument. Let S be an infinite subset of the whole numbers. The set of whole numbers has a least element, 0 and every subset of the whole numbers has a least element. So S has a least element. Now suppose that some element of S, say g, is the greatest element. Then there are a finite number of elements between the least element and g. But S has an infinite number of elements. So the set S must contain other elements that are not between the least element and g. These elements are greater than g. Thus the set S has no greatest element.

11. The subsets of {a,b,c,d} are:{ }, {a}, {b}, {c}, {d}, {a,b}, {a,c}, {a,d}, {b,c}, {b,d}, {c,d}, {a,b,c}, {a,b,d}, {a,c,d}, {b,c,d}, {a,b,c,d}.

13. All sets that are in a one-to-one correspondence are defined as equivalent sets and are associated with the same whole number. All empty sets are equivalent and are associated with the least of the whole numbers, 0. If the removal of a single element from one of a group of equivalent sets leaves that set equivalent to the empty set, then the remaining sets of the group are associated with the number 1. If the removal of a single element from one of a group of equivalent sets leaves that set equivalent to a set associated with the number 1, then the remaining sets of the group are associated with the number 2. This argument may be continued throughout the whole numbers.

15. The sets A = {a,b,c,d}, B = {w,x,y,z}, and C = {a,b,y,z} are all equivalent to the set S = {a,b,c,d}.
   a. Sets C and S show that equivalent sets do not necessarily have all elements in common.
   b. Sets B and S show that equivalent sets do not necessarily have any elements in common.
   c. Equivalent sets must have the same NUMBER of elements.

17. a. The empty set is the only subset of itself.
    b. The empty set has no proper subsets because it is the only subset of itself.
    c. One can conclude that there is no whole number less than the number associated with the empty set, the number 0.

19. a. **False**: equivalent sets are not necessarily equal because, although the numbers of elements are equal in the two sets, the actual elements may differ.
    b. **True**: if two sets do not contain the same number of elements they cannot contain exactly the same elements.
    c. **True**: if two sets contain exactly the same elements those sets contain the same numbers of elements
    d. **False**. Although A and B may not contain exactly the same elements, they may contain the same NUMBER of elements.

21. The librarian means that although faculty may check out new books, they may check out only some, not all, of the newly acquired books.

23. The elements of the sets W and N may be paired: 0-1, 1-2, 2-3, 3-4, 4-5, ..., (n-1)-n, n-(n+1),...

25. Let the persons available to serve on the committee comprise the set S = {A, B, C, D, E}. A subcommittee must contain at least one person and may be a committee of the whole. So the number of possible subcommittees (see question 11) is the number of subsets of S excluding the empty set: $2^4 - 1 = 16 - 1 = 15$

27. Responses will vary. Possibilities include: sets of students and sets of desks, persons invited to a party and party favors, plates and persons at the dinner table. Some problems are trivial such as more Christmas cards than stamps; others more serious as more children than doses of vaccine.

SECTION 2.2

1. a. This statement is true for the **numeral 8**.
   b. This is true for the **number** 4.
   c. This statement refers to the given **numerals**.

3. a. The number 408 would be represented with 4 'hundreds' squares, 0 'tens' sticks, and 8 'units' cubes.
   b. $3699 = \mathbf{3(1000) + 6(100) + 9(10) + 9(1)}$.
   c. $5{,}280{,}492 = \mathbf{5(10^6) + 2(10^5) + 8(10^4) + 0(10^3) + 4(10^2) + 9(10^1) + 2(10^0)}$.

5. a. The base-ten representation is $3(25) + 4(4) + 4(1) = \mathbf{99}$.
   b. The base-ten representation is $2(9) + 0(3) + 2(1) = \mathbf{20}$.
   c. The base-ten representation is $1(64) + 0(32) + 1(16) + 0(8) + 0(4) + 1(2) + 1(1) = \mathbf{83}$.

7. As described in the text: "...a tally system is based on establishing a one-to-one correspondence between a single mark and a single object so that the marks represent the number of objects. Later the idea of using grouping to simplify a numeration system emerged."

9.

	100	61	608	94
a. Egyptian	ρ	∩∩∩∩∩|	ρρρρρρ||||||||	∩∩∩∩∩∩∩∩∩||||
b. Babylonian	▼ << <<	▼ ▼	< ▼▼▼▼ ▼▼▼▼	▼ <<< ▼▼▼▼
c. Roman	C	LXI	DCVIII	XCIV

11. Various students will approach this question with different degrees of rigor.
    a. Egyptian numeration is based on a grouping system of powers of ten. One of each power of ten is represented by a different symbol and a number is represented with the fewest number of symbols. The Hindu-Arabic system is also based on powers of ten but is a place value rather than a grouping system.
    b. All students should note that both the Babylonian and Hindu-Arabic systems are place value systems although they use different bases. The Hindu-Arabic system has a different symbol for each numeral representing numbers from zero through ten. The Babylonian numeration system uses a modified tally and grouping system within the places.
    c. There are few similarities between the Roman and the Hindu-Arabic numeration systems. The Roman system is unique in that it utilizes both additive and subtractive relations. The Roman system also uses a grouping symbolism similar to the Egyptian.

13.

BASE-TEN NUMERALS

```
 1   2   3   4   5   6   7   8   9  10
11  12  13  14  15  16  17  18  19  20
21  22  23  24  25  26  27  28  29  30
31  32  33  34  35  36  37  38  39  40
41  42  43  44  45  46  47  48  49  50
51  52  53  54  55  56  57  58  59  60
61  62  63  64  65  66  67  68  69  70
71  72  73  74  75  76  77  78  79  80
81  82  83  84  85  86  87  88  89  90
91  92  93  94  95  96  97  98  99 100
```

    a. To find 10 more than a number go down one row in the same column.
    b. To find 10 less than a number go up one row in the same column.
    c. To find one more than a number move one space to the right or, if at the end of a row, go to the first space in the next row.
    d. To find one less than a number move one space to the left or, if at the left end of the row, go to the far right space in the above row.
    e. To find 11 more than a number move one row down and one space right.
    f. To find eleven less than a number move one row up and one space left.
    g. To find 9 more than a number move one row down and then one space left.
    h. To find 9 less than a number move one row up and then one space right.

15. The numeral $rstu_b$ may be expanded to: $u(b^0) + t(b^1) + s(b^2) + r(b^3)$.

17. a. The count of each set of symbols was multiplied by the value of the symbol. These products were then summed to obtain the base-ten numeral.
    b. The numerals in each place were summed as in part a and then these values were multiplied by the appropriate power of 60. Finally, these values were summed to obtain the base-ten value.

c.   The Roman numerals were grouped into sets of the same symbol and pairs of different symbols. If the different symbols decreased left to right their values were added. If the different symbols increased left to right the smaller was subtracted from the larger. Values of groups of the same symbol were multiplied by the number of symbols in the set. Finally, all these values were summed to obtain the base-ten representation.

19.   Although creative students may suggest ways of extending place value blocks past the b^3 place, the usefulness of this manipulative is generally restricted to the b^3 place.

21.   BASE-FIVE CHART   BASE-TEN CHART
      1   2   3   4   10
      11   12   13   14   20   SEE
      21   22   23   24   30   THE BASE-TEN CHART
      31   32   33   34   40   IN PROBLEM 13
      41   42   43   44   100
      The patterns identified in the two charts should be essentially the same.

23.   The responses to this question depend upon the imaginations of the students.

25.   Assume that there are 10 hamburgers to a foot. Then 400 billion hamburgers would form a stack about 40 billion feet high. Assuming 5000 feet per a mile, the 40 billion (40 000 000 000) feet high stack is about 8 million miles high. This distance is about 32 times the earth-moon distance or about one twelfth the earth-sun distance. So the correct answer is **e**.

27.   Responses to this question depend on the prior mathematical and educational experiences of students and upon their willingness to do research.

29.   The base-ten number represented by the numeral 421 could be represented as **645**$_{eight}$; that is 6 groups of 64 plus 4 groups of 8 plus 5 units. If the base is to be 16, then additional symbols are required. A base 16 system similar to base ten requires 16 separate symbols. These commonly are, in counting order, 0, 1, 2, 3, 4, 5, 6, 7, 8, 9, A, B, C, D, E, F. Thus 421 = **1A5**$_{sixteen}$. This numeral is 1 group of 256 plus A =10_{ten} groups of 16 plus 5 units.

SECTION 2.3

1.   a.   {@,@,@,@,@,@,@,@} ∪ {$,$,$,$,$,$,$,$} = {@,@,@,@,@,@,@,@,$,$,$,$,$,$,$,$}.
     b.   { } ∪ {&,&,&,&,&,&,&,&,&,&} = {&,&,&,&,&,&,&,&,&,&}.
     c.   Show the union between 2 disjoint set, one with 123 elements and the other with 324 elements.

3.   a.   The union is E = {those people who are either more than 20 years old or those persons enrolled in college (or both)}.
     b.   The union is C = {10, 20, 30, 40}
     c.   The union is G = {1,2,3,4,5,6,....., 98,99,100,102,104,106,....}.

5.   Responses will vary. Some examples are:
     a.   If 2000 tickets to a concert were pre-sold and another 356 were sold at the door, how many tickets total were sold?
     b.   If 2000 miles were traveled on the interstate and 356 miles on secondary roads, what total distance was covered?

7.   Examples will vary.
   a.   This is an application of the **commutative** property of addition: $2 + 8 = 8 + 2$.
   b.   This is an application of the **identity** property of addition: $a + 0 = 0 + a = a$.
   c.   This is an application of the **associative** property of addition:
        $8 + 7 = 1 + 7 + 7 = 1 + (7 + 7) = 1 + 14 = 15$.
   d.   This is an application of the **uniqueness** property of sums.

9.   a. $\{x,x,x,x,x,x,x,x,a,a,a,a,a,a,a,a\} - \{a,a,a,a,a,a,a,a\} = \{x,x,x,x,x,x,x,x\}$
   b. $\{a,a,a,a,a,a,a,a,a,a\} - \{a,a,a,a,a,a,a,a,a,a,\} = \{\ \}$.
   c. $\{1,2,3,4,...,445,446,447\} - \{1,2,3,4,...321,322,323,324\} = \{325,326,327,...445,446,447\}$.

11.   The definition of subtraction is: $a - b = c$ iff there exists a unique whole number, c, such that $a = b + c$.
   a. $18 - 8 = n$ is equivalent to $\mathbf{18 = n + 8}$.
   b. $25 - x = 15$ is equivalent to $\mathbf{25 = 15 + x}$.
   c. $\mathbf{y = 129 + 83}$.
   d. $\mathbf{a^2 = 30 + a}$.

13.   The responses to this question will vary among students. Some representative responses are:
   a.   A student had 12 lottery tickets. Five of these were known losers. How many tickets remained?
   b.   To complete a project, Sue had to take a 12 foot board and cut it into two pieces in the ratio of 7 to 5. How long should each piece be?
   c.   A professor has 2 quizzes, one with 12 questions, the other with five. If the questions are of equal difficulty, which will take a student longer to complete?
   d.   If a five foot piece is cut from a 12 foot board, how much of the original board remains?
   e.   How many questions should be added to the professor's 5 question quiz on part b so that the quiz will have 12 questions?

15.   a.   The key sequence would be:$\mathbf{+\ 1 = = +\ 10 = = = = +\ 100 = = =}$.
   b.   The display would be: $\mathbf{1, 2, 12, 22, 32, 42, 142, 242, 342}$.
   c.   The properties of **commutativity and associativity** are applied.

17.   a.   The set of odd whole numbers is not closed under addition. For example, $3 + 5 = 8$.
   b.   The natural numbers are a subset of the whole numbers that lacks an additive identity element.
   c,d. These subsets of the whole numbers do not exist.

19.   a.   The properties used are associativity and base-ten place value: $9 + 6 = 9 + (1 + 5) = (9 + 1) + 5 = 10 + 5$. But in base-ten, 10 is represents by a '1' in the second position. Thus $10 + 5$ is represented as 15.
   b.   The response to this question depends upon the insights of the students. A possibility is: the sums of $1000 + 500$, $100 + 50$, and $10 + 5$ have the same non-zero digits.

21. $24_{five} < 30_{five}$ because $24_{five} + 1_{five} = 30_{five}$.

23.   Responses will vary among students. Students might point out that subtraction problems can be rewritten as missing addend addition relations. Separating a set into two sets in modeled by physically removing objects from some set. The objects removed may be placed into a one-to-one correspondence with some third set. Thus 2 sets are formed: one from the objects removed and the other by the objects that remain.   When comparing sets one may remove objects from the two sets in pairs, one from each set, to determine which, if either, has elements remaining after one of the sets has been reduced to the null set.

25. a. If a increases or c decreases, then e increases. When a decreases or c increases, then e decreases. If a increases and c decreases, e increases.
    b. Tests applied will vary among students.
    c. See part a.
    d. e decreases if: a decreases, c increases, a increases by less than c increases, a decreases by more than c decreases. e increases if: a increases, c decreases, a increases by more than c increases, a decreases by less than c decreases.
    e. Responses depend on interactions among students.

27. **False**. The set {0} is a finite set of whole numbers and $0 + 0 = 0$.

29. Responses may vary. One possibility is

#	a	b	c	d
a	a	b	c	d
b	b	c	d	a
c	c	d	a	b
d	d	a	b	c

This system is analogous to addition mod 4.

31. a. If the proviso $k > 0$ were omitted but we still stay in the set of whole numbers, we have the situation that although a equals a, $a + 0 = a$ which implies that a is greater than a.
    b. The definition of 'less than' might be stated: a is less than b iff there exists some whole number $k > 0$ such that $a = b - k$.

33. Responses will vary. Possible ideas are: Scribes might have treated subtraction as missing addend problems. Suppose the Scribe wanted to determine the difference 14 -6. Interpreting the problem as $14 = 6 + ?$ the scribe would locate that 14 in the body of the table that had one addend of 6 and find the corresponding other addend.

SECTION 2.4

1. To verify the operations one would:
    a. show the union of 12 disjoint sets each with three elements.
    b. show the union of 14 empty sets.
    c. show the union of three disjoint sets each with 100 elements.

3. Answers will vary among students. Representative responses might be:
    a. If each of 4 children received 30 pieces of candy on Halloween and put all the candy in a bag to share with their classmates, how many pieces of candy were in the bag?
    b. If 4 students are running a relay in which each student runs 30 meters, how long in the race?

5. a. Let L represent the number of lunches: L = 5 soup x 8 salad = **40** soup-salad.
    b. Let O represent the number of outfits: O = 8 blouse x 4 skirt x 4 vest = **128** blouse-skirt-vest
    c. Let w represent the number of wrapping paper types and c the number of bow colors. Then w x c = 72.

7. a. Multiplication is **commutative**: a x b = b x a.
    b   There is a **zero property** of multiplication: for each whole number a, a x 0 = 0 x a = 0.
    c. In the whole numbers multiplication is **distributive** over addition. Suppose that c + 1 = b.
        Then a x b = a x (c + 1) = ac + a.
    d. The whole numbers are **closed** under multiplication: the product of 2 whole numbers is a unique whole
        number.
    e. The place value of a digit in the base-ten system is 10 times the value it would have were it in the next
        right hand place.

9. Responses will vary among students. Representative responses are:
    a. A teacher has a bank of 24 test questions and wishes to create tests with 6 questions. How many tests are
        possible?
    b. A shop teacher cut a 24 inch piece of wire into 6 inch segments. How many pieces were cut?
    c. A teacher has a bank of 24 test questions and wishes make 6 tests with the same number of questions.
        How many questions will be on each test?
    d. A shop teacher had a piece of wire 24 inches long. He bent the wire into 6 pieces of equal length. How
        long was each straight piece?
    e. A teacher made 6 tests with the same number of questions. The total number of questions was 24. How
        many questions were on each test?

11. a. $18 = 6 \times n; n = \mathbf{3}$.
    b. $25 = 5 \times X; X = \mathbf{5}$.
    c. $y = 42 \times 126; y = \mathbf{5292}$.
    d. $\mathbf{0 = b \times c}$. c = 0 (b cannot be 0 because it is the denominator of the original expression.   Thus b is any
        natural number.)

13. a. $19 \div 3 = \mathbf{6\ r\ 1}$ because 6(3) + 1 = 19.
    b. $256 \div 20 = \mathbf{12\ r\ 16}$ because 20(12) + 16 = 256.
    c. $2 \div 8 = \mathbf{0\ r\ 2}$ because 0(8) + 2 = 2.

15. Predictions will vary among students.

	predicted n(C)	C	actual n(C)
a.	3	{(a,r),(b,r),(c,r)}	**3**
b.	8	{(1,a),(1,b),(2,a),(2,b),(3,a),(3,b),(4,a),(4,b)}	**8**
c.	0	{ } (there are no elements in { } to pair with elements of the second set. Thus there are no ordered pairs and C is empty.	**0**

    d. $3 \times 1 = 3; 4 \times 2 = 8; 0 \times 6 = 0$.

17. To determine the value of a particular place within the numeral the appropriate power of 10 is multiplied by
    the face value of that place.

19. a. $2a + 2b = \mathbf{2(a + b)}$.
    b. $14 r + 18r^2 = \mathbf{2r(7 + 9r)}$.
    c. $6c + 12d + 15e = \mathbf{3(2c + 4d + 5e)}$.

21. Responses will vary among students. They might be based upon the concept that division problems can be
    rewritten as 'missing factor' problems. The table can be used to find the missing factor.

23. a.. If the values of q and r that satisfy (q x 15) + r = 95 are restricted to the whole numbers, the (q,r) pairs are: (0,95), (1,80), (2,65), (3,50), (4,35), (5,20), (6,5).
     b. Only the pair q = 6, r = 5 satisfy the division algorithm because when dividing 95 by 15 the quotient must be less than 15 and the remainder must be less than the quotient.
     c. If the restriction were dropped any of the above (q,r) pairs would satisfy the division algorithm and the quotient would not be unique.

25. The responses to this questions will vary among students and will depend on the insights developed by the students. Students may notice that the table is symmetric with respect to the upper-left to lower-right diagonal because of the commutative property.

27. **Yes, it could be true**. When there were 4 candy dishes the possible remainders were 0, 1, 2, 3. If these occurred with equal frequency, then Eleanor ate an average of one and a half pieces of candy for each bag. But with 7 dishes , the possible remainders are 0, 1, 2, 3, 4, 5, 6 which gives an average of 3 candies left after filling the dishes.

29. **All these sets are closed under multiplication**. First consider the set of even whole numbers. 0 times any element is 0 and therefore is in the set. A whole number is even iff it has a factor of 2. Thus the product of 2 even numbers is even because the product has a factor of 2. A similar argument holds for a set of multiples of 3. Now consider the odd whole numbers. An odd number is an even plus 1: O = E + 1. So the product of 2 odd numbers is: (E + 1)x (E + 1) = EE + (E + E) + 1. Now, EE is even and the sum of evens is even. So EE + E + E is even. Adding 1 to this sum results in an odd number. For parts d and e we see that 1 x 1 = 1 and 0 x 0 = 0.

31. a. $0 \div a = 0$ because this is equivalent to 0 = a x 0 which is true for all a not equal to 0 by the definition of the zero property.
     b. Suppose $a \div 0$ were defined and had a quotient c. We could rewrite it as a multiplication relation: $a \div 0$ = c becomes a = c x 0 = 0. But c could be any whole number and a quotient, by definition, is unique.
     c. Suppose $0 \div 0$ were defined and had a whole number quotient c. Then, by definition of division and quotient, c is a unique whole number. So $0 \div 0$ = c; or 0 = c x 0. But this would be true for all whole numbers. But the quotient of two whole numbers is unique. Thus $0 \div 0$ is undefined.

33. This questions requires student interaction and activity.

35. To bring closure to the whole numbers under division we must expand the set of numbers to include the rational numbers. They are useful in situations in which a unit is to be distributed to a number of individuals. The whole numbers are a subset of the rational numbers. The quotient of any 2 whole numbers, if defined, exists within the set of rational numbers.

CHAPTER 2 REVIEW EXERCISES

1. a. The following sets have '5' in common: {#,#,#,#,#}. {<,<,<,<,<}, {*,*,*,*,*}, {$,$,$,$,$}, {1,2,3,4,5}.
    b. Let N = {$,$,$,$,$,$,$,$,$} and E = {@,@,@,@,@,@,@,@,@,@,@}. Since N is equivalent to a proper subset of E, n(N) < n(E) or 9 < 11.
    c. The sets { }, { }, { } show the meaning of 0.
    d. Since { } is equivalent to a proper subset of any non-empty set, 0 < all other whole numbers.

3.   Responses will vary among students. responses might include;
   a.   The Egyptian numeration system is a tally system through 9 of a symbol with a different symbol for every power of 10. Early numeration had no 0 symbol.
   b.   The Babylonian system is a place value system based on powers of 60. It incorporates a tally system of 2 symbols tallying units to 9 and tens to fifty.
   c.   The Roman system uses different symbols for units, tens, fifties, hundreds, five hundreds, and thousands. It employs both additive and subtractive characteristics to keep the number of repetitions of a symbol to 3 or less.
   d.   The Hindu-Arabic system is a place value system based on powers of 10. It uses different symbols for the numbers 0 through 9.

5.   a, b. Student activities. For example, to represent 1208 use 1 thousands cube, 2 flats, no sticks and 8 units.
   c. $1208 = 1(1000) + 2(100) + 0(10) + 8(1)$.
   d. $1208 = 1(10^3) + 2(10^2) + 0(10^1) + 8(10^0)$.

7.   Responses will vary. Examples are:
   a.   How much fencing is needed to enclose plots with perimeters 85 inches and 62 inches?
   b.   Joe got 85 pledges for a hunger walk and Jan got 62 pledges. If there were no persons who pledged to both Joe and Jan, how many people pledged to both Joe and Jan?

9.   Responses will vary. Examples are:
   a.   To make 3 square frames, an artist needs 12 strips of material. If she has 25 displays each requiring 3 frames, how many strips are necessary?
   b.   Each of 12 students brings 25 candies to class. How many candies were brought to class?
   c.   A rectangle is 12 by 25 inches. What is the area of this rectangle?
   d.   Joe has 12 shirts and 25 ties. How many different combinations of shirt and tie may he select from?

11.   The set of flowers may be represented {a,b,c,d}. A student may use some or all of the flowers, a subset of the set of flowers, but no student may use no flowers in an arrangement. There are 15 subsets of a 4 element set, excluding the null set. So the 15 students can each make a different arrangement.

13. $80 - 159 = 121$ because $180 = 59 + 121$.

15.   a.   **S is closed** under addition because the sum of multiples of 10 is a multiple of 10.
   b.   The **additive identity is 0** because any element of the set added to 0 results in the original element.
   c.   The set is **closed under multiplication** because the set is multiples of 10 and if a multiple of 10 is multiplied by any whole number not 0, then the product contains a factor of ten and thus is a multiple of 10.
   d.   The set **does not have** an element such that multiplication of any element by this elements results in the original element.
   e.   The **associative, commutative, and distributive properties do apply** to S.

17. $125 \div 40 = $ **3 r 5** because $3 \times 40 + 5 = 125$.

19. The drawings will vary among students. They should represent the relation that sets are in a one-to-one correspondence if the elements of one set can be paired with elements of another set. If the pairing can produce pairs of identical elements the sets are called equal.

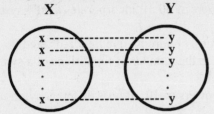

If each element of X can be paired be paired with an element of Y then the sets are in a 1 to 1 correspondence, represent the same whole number, and are equivalent.   If, further, each element of X can be paired with an identical element in Y, the sets are equal.

21. Responses this question depend upon interactions within groups of students.

SECTION 3.1

1. a. Compatible pairs of numbers are 12 and 18 (sum = 30 by inspection) , 46 and 64 (sum = 110 by inspection). So, applying the commutative and associative properties of addition one gets: $12 + 46 + 18 + 64 = 12 + 18 + 46 + 64 = 30 + 110 = \mathbf{140}$.
    b. Applying the commutative and associative properties: $5 \times 18 \times 4 = (5 \times 4) \times 18 = 20 \times 18 = \mathbf{360}$.
    c. As in part b, one gets: $25 \times 28 \times 4 = (25 \times 4) \times 28 = 100 \times 28 = \mathbf{2800}$.
    d. Applying the associative property we get: $60 + 140 + 39 + 51 = (60 + 140) + (39 + 51) = 200 + 90 = \mathbf{290}$.

3. a. To compute 848 - 300 one need only count back by one hundred three times: 848, 748 (back 1), 648 (back 2), 548 (back 3). So the result is **548**.
    b. To compute 458 + 20 one counts on by ten twice: 458, 468 (on 1), **478** (on 2).
    c. To compute 648 + 32, first one counts on by ten three times and then twice in the units place: 648, 658, 668, 678, 679, **680**.
    d. To compute 927 - 30, one counts back by ten three times: 927, 917, 907, **897**.

5. a. Apply the associative property: $(85 + 12 + 18) = 85 + (12 + 18) = 85 + 30$. Now count by ten three times: 85, 95, 105, **115**.
    b. Apply the associative property: $(28 \cdot 5) \cdot 2 = 28 \cdot (5 \cdot 2) = 28 \cdot 10 = \mathbf{280}$.
    c. Reverse the distributive property [factor]: $(18 \cdot 6) - (15 \cdot 6) = (18 - 15) \cdot 6 = 3 \cdot 6 = \mathbf{18}$.
    d. Apply the associative property: $(186+67) + 33 = 186 + (67+33) = 186 + 100$. Now count on by 100 once: 186, **286**.

7. The techniques will vary among students. Some possible techniques are:
    a. Associative property and compatible numbers: $12 \cdot (40 \cdot 5) = 12 \cdot 200 = \mathbf{2400}$.
    b. Reverse the distributive property: $7 \cdot 14 + 3 \cdot 14 = (7 + 3) \cdot 14 = 10 \cdot 14 = \mathbf{140}$.
    c. Break apart, commutative and associative properties: $53 + 26 = 50 + 3 + 20 + 6 = (50 + 20) + (3 + 6) = 70 + 9 = \mathbf{79}$.
    d. Break apart and distributive property: $45 \cdot 5 = (40 + 5) \cdot 5 = 40 \cdot 5 + 5 \cdot 5 = 200 + 25 = \mathbf{225}$.
    e. Commutative and associative properties and compatible numbers: $24 + 39 + 76 = (24 +76) + 39 = 100 + 39 = \mathbf{139}$.
    f. Use compensation, first add one 17, then subtract one 17: $9 \cdot 17 = 10 \cdot 17 - 17 = 170 - 17 = \mathbf{153}$.
    g. Use compensation: add 1 then subtract 1. $147 - 38 = 147 + 1 - 38 - 1 = 148 - 38 - 1 = 110 - 1 = \mathbf{109}$.
    h. Count on in the tens place: 488, 498, 508, **518**.
    i. Use compensation: add 1 then subtract . $455 - 26 = 455 + 1 - 26 - 1 = 456 - 26 - 1 = 430 - 1 = \mathbf{429}$.
    j. Use the commutative and associative properties to get compatible numbers: $6 \cdot 22 \cdot 5 = (6 \cdot 5) \cdot 22 = 30 \cdot 22 = \mathbf{660}$.

9. Responses will vary among students. A possiblity is: $542+45=540+2+40+5=540+40+2+5=580+7= 587$.

11. Carly's thinking **is not correct**. When she subtracted 40, she subtracted 2 too many. Thus to compensate she must add 2, not subtract 2 more. So she should reason: to obtain the difference between 126 and 38, I'll first subtract 40, which is taking away 2 too many, getting 86. Now to compensate for taking away 2 too many, I'll add 2 getting 88.

13. The total price for a queen set and a twin set from W. S. Manufacturing is $\$119 + 2(\$33)$ and the total price for the same two sets from Royalty Premier is $\$499 + 2(\$179)$. So: $(499+358) - (119 +66) = (500-120)+(362-70) = 380 + (370 - 70) - 8 = 680 - 8 = 672$. The difference in total price is **\$672**.

15. The difference in average weekly spending between 18-19 year-old and 12-14 year-old students is $\$81.24 - \$36.25 = 81.25 - 31.25 - 5 - .01 = \mathbf{\$44.99}$.

17. Answers will vary among students. Possible responses are:
   a. First use an under-estimate: 28 times 20 is 560, more than 500. So the answer is 'yes'.
   b. An exact answer is required. Although mental computations could be used, either pencil and paper or calculator computations are appropriate to find the difference: 365.25 - 48.89.
   c. An exact answer is called for. The data is such that mental computation by break-apart into compatible numbers is an appropriate method. $34 + 46 + 52 + 38 = (30 + 40) + (50 + 30) + (4 + 6) + (2 + 8) = 170$.
   d. An exact answer is called for. It mat be determined as: $30 \times 150 = (3 \times 15) \times 10 \times 10 = 4500$.
   e. Because the actual questions asks "... about how much..", only an estimate is required. Mental computations are appropriate. Estimate the cost per tire as $50.
   f. An exact answer is called for. Pencil and paper computations or a fraction calculator are appropriate to find the produce (10) (3 1/4 + 2 1/2 + 2 3/4).

19. Responses to this question depend upon the knowledge and insights of the students. Responses might include: Persons with poor understanding of place value may not be able to apply counting on when carrying is required. For example, the sum of $287 + 30$ requires counting on: 287, 297, 307, 317. Person with poor understanding of place value may have difficulty in separating a number into place values such as: to determine the product of 8 and 28, one might improperly use the techniques of adding 8 times 2 and 8 times 8 rather than adding 8 times 20 and 8 times 8.

21. Responses will vary among students. Possible responses are:
   a. One might have a symbolism that directly permits 42 to be separated into $40 + 1 + 1$ just by spacing the symbols. One '1' could then be appended to the '39' resulting in the addition of 40 and 40. The remaining one could then be appended.
   b. A similar symbolism might permit the appending of a '5' symbol to each numeral producing an equivalent but simpler computation: 2940 - 1500.

SECTION 3.2

1. a. 6783 rounds to **6780.** Since 3 is < 5, replace it with a 0.
   b. 26.09 rounds to **26.1.** Since $9 \geq 5$ the place to the ieft is incremented. So the 0 becomes a 1.
   c. 209.8 rounds to **210.** Since $8 \geq 5$, the place to the left is incremented.
   d. 2995 rounds to **3000.** Since $9 \geq 5$, increment the place to the left and fill the places to the right with 0's.
   e. 851 rounds to **900.**   Since $5 \geq 5$, this is the same as part d.
   f. 749.9 rounds to 750. This is the same as parts d and e.

3. Responses will vary. Possible responses are:
   a. Replace $424 + 526$ with $425 + 525$ and obtain the result **950**.
   b. Replace $1195 - 195$ with $1200 - 200$. The result is **1000**.
   c. Replace $23 \cdot 8$ with $20 \cdot 10$. The estimated result is **200**.
   d. Replace $430 \div 6.8$ with $420 \div 7$ and obtain the estimate **60**.

5. Answers may vary among students. Possible responses include:
   a. $824 + 238$ is approximated by $(800 + 200) + (20 + 40) = 1000 + 60 = $ **1060**.
   b. $23,869 + 14,198$ is approximated by $(20\ 000 + 10\ 000) + (4\ 000 + 4\ 000) = $ **38,000**.
   c. $38 + 64 + 46 + 76 + 87$ can be approximated by $(30 + 60 + 40 + 70 + 80) + (10+10+10) = $ **310**.
   d. $7,653 - 2,861$ can be approximated by $(7,000 - 2,000) + 600 - 800 = $ **4,800**.

7. Responses will vary. Student responses might include:
    a. The product 54×38 is between $50 \times 30 = \textbf{1500}$ and $60 \times 40 = \textbf{2400}$.
    b. A range is $700 + 800 = \textbf{1,500}$ to $800 + 900 = \textbf{1,700}$.
    c. A range for the difference is $(600 - 200) = \textbf{400 to } (700 - 100) = \textbf{600}$.
    d. A range is $20 \times 9 = \textbf{180}$ to $25 \times 10 = \textbf{250}$.

9. Responses will vary among students. Possible responses include:
    a. Using rounding: $25,000 + 66,000 = 91,000$. The exact answer is greater. The estimate is low because one addend was rounded down more that the other was rounded up. The exact sum is **91,335.**
    b. Using compatible numbers we get the estimate $1000 \times 60 = 60,000$. The exact product is greater because one factor was reduced by a greater percentage (66 to 60 is about a 10% reduction) than the other was increased (978 to 1000 is about a 3% increase).   The exact product is **64,548**.
    c. Using clustering we get an estimation of $4 \times 800 = 3200$. Because the numbers less than the cluster number are farther from the cluster number than those greater, the exact result, **3165**, is less.
    d. With compatible numbers we get an estimate of $50 \times 20 = 1,000$. Since each compatible factor is less than the actual factor it replaces, the exact product, **1,242**, is greater.
    e. Using rounding we estimate $700 \div 70 = 10.$. But since $700 < 726$ and $70 > 67$, the exact answer, **10.8**, is greater that the estimate.
    f. Using compatible numbers we get the estimate $10 \times 26 = 260$. Since $10 < 12$, the exact product, **312**, is greater than the estimate.

11. Responses will vary among students. Possible responses include: If the estimator employed the compatible number technique, a possible factor is 48. If rounding was the technique of choice, the other factor could be any number between 45 and 54.

13. Harvey knows that $8,000 - 3,000$ is $5,000$ and notes that the difference between 8,000 and 7,653 is greater than the difference between 3,000 and 2,861. So the over-estimate of 7,653 is greater than the over-estimate of 2,861. Over-estimating the minuend produces a large estimate, over-estimating the subtrahend produces a small estimate. Since the over-estimate of the minuend is greater than the over-estimate of the subtrahend, the overall **estimate (5,000) is larger** than the exact difference.

15. Responses will vary among students. Possible responses include: the sum of 238 and 273 is approximately 500. Use 250 as a cluster number. The product of 21 and 26 is approximately 500. Use the compatible numbers 20 and 25.

17. Responses will vary among students. A possible argument is: Were I Victoria, I would overestimate the cost so I would be sure of having the cash upon demand. So I would estimate: $40 \times 25 = \$1,000$.

19. Responses will vary among students. A possible response is: a slight overestimate would be appropriate. If the amount is overestimated, the concrete company will bring an excess. It may be easier to dispose of the excess than pay for another trip to make up the difference between what is required and an underestimated amount.

21. Responses will vary among students. A possible response is: Use front-end estimation. Four times 22 million is 88 million.

23. Answers will vary among students. Using rounding we get the difference $76\% - 24\% = 52\%$.

25. Responses to this question depend on student activities. Some responses might be: Estimation is used to predict grades, determine travel times to and from campus, decide if sufficient money is available among a few friends to attend some activity.

27. Responses to this question depend upon interactions among students in the class.

SECTION 3.3

1.

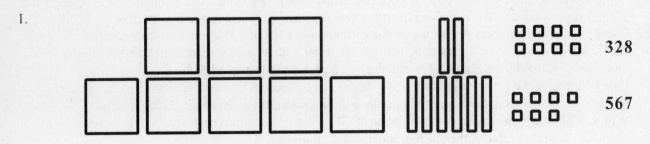

3.   The properties are, in order: **associative, commutative, associative, distributive**.

5.   Responses will vary in the manner in which the error is described and base-ten blocks are used to illustrate the errors. Possible responses include:
   a.   The error is in subtracting the smaller place value from the larger ignoring which is the subtrahend and which is the minuend.
   b.   The error is not executing the trade of 1 'ten' for 10 'ones' in the minuend. Ten extra units were added to the units place but the tens place was not reduced by the corresponding amount.
   c.   There are several errors. As above, although the ones place of the minuend was increased by ten units the tens place was not reduced by one ten. It appears that the hundreds place was reduced and when hundreds were subtracted the zero place holder in the difference was not inserted.
   d.   The units numbers and the tens numbers were added separately. 7 units and 5 units are indeed 1 ten and 2 units. But this ten was not added to the tens already present. The tens were treated as a separate units problem. Place value in the original addends was ignored.

7.   Jorge neglected to included the parentheses in his computation.

9.   Responses will vary. Two possibilities are: boots (137), cooking utensils (47), and trail food (12) for a total of $196 or rain gear (89), stove (68), and cooking utensils (47) for a total of $194.

11. Responses will vary among students. All should, however, address regrouping. In the first illustration the student regrouped the number 204 (2 hundreds, 0 tens, and 4 ones) into 1 hundred, 10 tens and 4 ones and then regrouped yet again into 1 hundred, 9 tens, and 14 ones. The student then proceeded to subtract place by place. In the second illustration the student regrouped both hundreds into 20 tens and then regrouped one of these tens into ones which left him with 19 tens. The regrouped 10 units was combined with the 4 units in the units place. Place by place subtraction then occurred.   The first is the standard algorithm. The second makes sense because the subtrahend has only tens and units.

13. a.   234 = 2 hundreds + 3 tens + 4 ones
            +125 = 1 hundred + 2 tens + 5 ones
                 = 3 hundreds + 5 tens + 9 ones
                 = 359

   b.   548 = 5 hundreds + 4 tens + 8 ones
            +276 = 2 hundreds + 7 tens   + 6 ones
                 = 7 hundreds + 11 tens + 14 ones
                 = 7 hundreds + 12 tens + 4 ones
                 = 8 hundreds + 2 tens   + 4 ones
                 = 824

c. 838 = 8 hundreds + 3 tens + 8 ones
  $+627$ = 6 hundreds + 2 tens + 7 ones
       = 14 hundreds + 5 tens + 15 ones
       = 14 hundreds + 6 tens +   5 ones
       = 1 thousand + 4 hundreds + 6 tens + 5 ones
       = 1465

d. 1256 = 1 thousand + 2 hundreds + 5 tens + 6 ones
  $+867$ =   8 hundreds + 6 tens + 7 ones
       = 1 thousand + 10 hundreds + 11 tens + 13 ones
       = 1 thousand + 10 hundreds + 12 tens + 3 ones
       = 1 thousand + 11 hundreds + 2 tens   + 3 ones
       = 2 thousand + 1 hundred + 2 tens   + 3 ones
       = 2123

15. a.   (Say-give): (13-0)(15-2) (20-5)(40-20)(60-20)(80-20)(85-5). So you have given 72. The difference is 72.
    b.   : (84-0)(85-1)(90-5)(100-10)(120-20)(130-10)(135-5). The difference is 51.
    c.   : (8-0)(10-2)(20-10)(24-4). The difference is 16.
    d.   : (32-0)(35-3)(55-20). The difference is 23.

17. Responses will vary. Possible responses include:
    a.   The solution first separates the addends into compatible numbers. $175 + 352 = 150 + 25 + 350 + 2$.
         Then the commutative property is applied: $150 + 25 + 350 + 2 = 150 + 350 + 25 + 2$.
         The associative property is used: $150 + 350 + 25 + 2 = (150 + 350) + (25 + 2) = 500 + 27 = 527$.
    b.   The addends are rewritten as: $175 + 352 = 100 + 75 + 300 + 52$.
         The commutative property is applied: $100 + 75 + 300 + 52 = 75 + 52 + 100 + 300$.
         Finally, the associative property is used: $(75 + 52) + (100 + 300) = 127 + 400 = 527$.
         An alternative explanation would be the application of front-end estimation and exact adjustment. Both
         approaches are valid.

19. Solutions will vary. A possible solution: the diggers net 50 m in a 24 hour period. So, at the end of the
    sixteenth day (the beginning of the seventeenth day) the shaft will be 800 m deep. At the end of the
    seventeenth day the shaft will be 850 m deep. So the 875 m mark will be reached one quarter into the
    eighteenth day of digging.

21. a.   By tracing out the routes we find 18 routes. Adding the mileage of some of these we get the following:
         ABCDEJK (1657), ACDEJK (1638), ABGFEJK (1339), ABGFIK (1256), ABGFIJK (1502), ABGHIK
         (1410),ABGHIJK (1656), ABCDEFGHIJK (2320).
    b.   The above data shows that **ABGFEJK** has a distance of **1339** miles and that **ABGFIK has a distance of
         1256 miles**.
    c.   Answers will vary. Another problem could be: What is the difference in distance between the shortest and
         longest routes?

23. a.   Using mental mathematics and compensation: 1349 - 875 = 1350 - 850 - 25 - 1 = `1300 - 800 -25 - 1 =
         500 - 25 - 1 = 475 - 1 = **474**.
    b.   Since the amount you must save is greater than $450 but less than $500 it will take over 9 months to save
         the money. If you credit yourself with savings on the last day of the month, it will take **10 months**.

25. Responses depend upon interactions among students. A possible response could be modeled on question #3.

27. Responses will vary. A possible example is: in the above problem we found that 645 - 268 = 377. We may
    check our subtraction by re-writing the subtraction relation as an addition equation: is it true that
    645 = 377 + 268? Since the answer is 'yes', the subtraction was correctly executed.

SECTION 3.4

1.

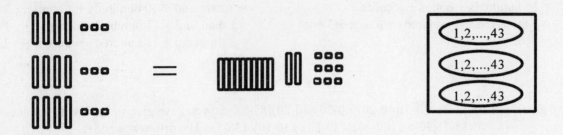

3. a. The partial products are 368 and 1380.
    b. The second partial product ends in 0 because the number of units in the product is completely in the first partial product. The 0 is "holding a place' until the partial products are added.
    c. Using rounding, an estimate is 40 x 50 = 2,000.

5. The basic computation was the multiplication of 12 x 22. The multiplicands were rewritten as sums, 22 x 12 = (10+10+1+1) x (10+1+1). Applying the distributive property we have:
    22 x 12 = (10+10+1+1) x (10+1+1) = (10 x 10 + 10 x 1 + 10 x 1 + 10 x 10 + 10 x 1 + 10 x 1 + 1 x 10 + 1 x 1 +1 x 1 + 1 x 10 + 1 x 1 + 1 x 1 = 264. The 2 10 by 10 products are the 2 large squares; the 6 10 by 1 products are the 6 rectangles; and 4 1 by 1 products are the 4 small squares.

7. Estimates will vary. A possible estimate is: changing to compatible numbers we approximate 4357 ÷ 32 with 4300 ÷ 43 = 100. A calculator gives 136 full groups of 32 in 4357.

9. a. Keystrokes: 2208, ÷, 12, ÷, 23, =, **8**
    b. Keystrokes: 34, x, 15, x, 364, ÷, 5, ÷, 52 = **714**.
    c. Keystrokes: 15, x, 12, ÷, 8 +, 124, = **147**

11. The highest score possible is 5 bull's eyes, 5 x 40 = **200 points**. The lowest score, assuming that all the darts score some points, is 5 outer rings, 5 x 10 = **50 points**.

13. Estimating 74 x 23 by mentally calculating with the compatible numbers 20 and 70 gives 1400, an estimate close to the (erroneously) computed value. Thus the estimate does not indicate an error in the computation. On the other hand, estimating 48x32 by rounding gives 50x30 = 1500. Since 220 is so far from 1500, the estimate indicates an error in the calculation.

15. First 45 is broken into addends, (40 + 5) and then the distributive property is applied.

17. Responses will vary. A possible explanation is; the person doing the computation is saying, albeit to him/herself: "My problem is to find out how many groups of 3 can be made from 86 items. OK, I'll start with making 15 groups of 3. This will take **15 x 3** = 45 of the 86 items leaving 41 to distribute in groups of 3. So I'll make another 12 groups of 3. This will take **12 x 3** = 36 of my 41 items leaving me with 5 to make into groups of 3. I can make 1 more group of three, taking **1 x 3** = 3 leaving me with 2 items that I cannot make into a group of 3. So I have made 15 + 12 + 1 = 28 groups of 3 using **28 x 3** = 84 of my original 86 items.

19 a. Divide $200,000 by $13000 using the approximation 225 ÷ 15= **15 years**.
    b. Compute 20 times the yearly difference with the adjusted calculation 20(40,000 - 25,000) = 20(15,000) = **$300 000.**
    c. The exact computation would be: Y = 13,000 ÷ (3% x 38,000). Estimate the number of years with the series of approximations: to get 1% of something, divide that amount by 100 which can be done by dropping 2 right-hand 0's. So 1% of 40,000 is 400. Thus 3% of 40,000 is 1200. So the teacher is saving about $1200 a year. So it will take about 13,000÷1300 = **13 years**. The exact computation is 13,000÷1140 = 11.4 years.
    d. Three times $23,000 is $69,000 in year 5. Now, in year 1 the driver makes $23,000, year 2 $23,000 + $8500, year 3 $23,000 + 17 000, and in year 4 $23,000 + $25,500 = $48,500. Thus in year 5 the driver must increase by the difference between $69,000 and $48,500: **$20 500.**

21. Responses will vary. Students may use a pure guess and check approach although some may see the value of using approximate square roots as starting points.
    a. Since the target is 50,000, begin with 200 x 200 because 200 squared is 40,000 and 300 squared is 90,000. Now try to narrow your possibility down by using a calculator 222 x 222 = 49 284.. 222 x 224 = 49,728. 221 x 226 = 49,946. Students may continue until satisfied.
    b. For 125,000 begin with 300 x 300. Try 311 x 311 = 96,721. Try 358 x 348 = 124,584. Continue until satisfied.

23. a. To save $1 million in 35 years, saving the same amount each year, one must save $1,000,000 ÷ 35 years = $28,571 per year. If this is one fourth yearly earnings, one must earn 4($28,571) = **$114,285** per year.
    b. Now, in this scenario, your spouse will contribute ($38,000 x 20) ÷ 3 = $253,333 to retirement leaving you to contribute $746,666 to your $1 million retirement fund. This is to be contributed over 35 years and is to be one third of your earnings, so your yearly earnings must be 3($746,666 ÷ 35) = **$64,000** per year.
    c. You want to obtain the sum: 75,000 + 200 + 400 + 800 + ... + 53,687,091,200 + 107,374,182,400. This can, of course, be done by brute force. One might note that the sum is also represented by: $S = 75,000 + 200(2^0 + 2^1 +... + 2^{29})$. This latter is a geometric series with first term 1, common ratio 2, and 30 terms. Some students may recall the sum of such a series is $1(1 - 2^{30})/1 - 2 = 1,073,741,823$. So the sum is approximately 75,000 + 200(1 billion) or about 200 billion dollars.

25. Responses will vary. We want the quotient of 486 and 15. We might estimate by first finding, mentally, 450 ÷ 15 = 30. The remaining 36 can be separated into 2 groups of 15, giving 32 bottles per carton with 6 left over.

27. In repeated subtraction you are removing subsets of a specific size and counting the number of subsets you can form. For example, how many 12's in 156? In sharing you begin with a number of subsets and determine the number of elements you can equally put in each. For example, If 156 things are to be equally shared among 12 individuals, how many does each individual recieve?

29. In short division the intermediate multiplications and subtractions are done mentally with only the differences recorded above and to the left of the next place to be considered in the division. In the example, 6 divides into 24 4 times (write this 4 in the partial quotient). Now, as in the standard algorithm, 6 times 4 is 24, and 24 from 28 is 4. Write this 4 above and left of the next dividend position, the 5. Continuing as in the standard algorithm: 6 divides into 45 7 times, write the 7 in the quotient. 7 times 6 is 42. Subtract 42 from 45 giving 3. Write the 3 above and left of the remaining (units) position. 6 divides into 30 5 times. Complete the quotient with the 5.

CHAPTER 3 REVIEW EXERCISES

1. a. 30, 80, 81, 82, 83, **84**.   b. 101, 100, **99**.
    c. 648, 548, **448**   d. 678, 778, **878**

3. a. 548 + 261 = 500 + 200 + 40 + 60 + 8 + 1 = 700 + 100 + 9 = **809**
    b. 826 - 125 = 800 - 100 + (26 - 25) = 700 + 1 = **701**
    c. 431 x 2 = 2 x (400 + 31) = 800 + 62 = **862**
    d. 648 ÷ 2 = (600 + 48) ÷ 2 = 600 ÷ 2 + 48 ÷ 2 = 300 + 24 = **324**

5. a. 48 - 27 = (48 + 2) - (27 + 2) = 50 - 29 = **21**
    b. 325 - 195 = (325 + 5) - (195 + 5) = 330 - 200 = **130**
    c. 210 - 88 = (210 + 2) - (88 + 2) = 212 - 90 = **122**
    d. 131 - 27 = (131 + 3) - (27 + 3) = 134 - 30 = **104**

7. a. 665 + 243, 700 + 200 = 900   b. 783 ÷ 4, 800 ÷ 4 = 200
    c. 75 x 12, 80 x 10 = 800   d. 704 - 337, 700 - 300 = 400

9. a. 436 + 735 = 1100 + 70 = 1170   b. 1243 + 5488 = 6000 + 700 = 6700
    c. 43 + 56 + 62 + 87 = 230 + 20 = 250   d. 43,650 + 45,436 = 88,000 + 1000 = 89,000

11. a. 2546 + 4337, estimate: 2500 + 4500 = 7000. Exact, **6883**
    b. 56 x 34, estimate: 60 x 30 = 1800. Exact: **1904**.
    c. 540 - 308, estimate: 540 - 300 = 240. Exact: **232**.
    d. 765 ÷ 4, estimate: 800 ÷ 4 = 200. Exact: **19.25**.

13.

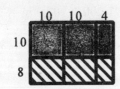

Half tone shading (▓) = **240**

Diagonal shading (◪) = **192**

15. Responses will vary. Responses may include the ideas: compatible numbers are numbers that are easy to compute with mentally. Different persons have different compatible numbers. Estimation is generally a mental process. For example, in adding groups of figures, 7 + 6 + 2 + 8 + 4 + 3 + 12 + 8 a common practice is to scan for pairs that add to 10.

17. There are 12 ÷ 2 possible pairs of jars: 4 choice for the first, 3 for the second: divided by 2 because the order of jars is not important.   The sums are (in thousands): 154+25=**179**, 154+750=**904**, 154+3.5=**157.5**, 25+750=**775**, 25+3.5=**28.5**, 750+3.5=**753.5**. The greatest difference is 904 - 28.5 = $875.5 K

19. Responses will vary. A possibility is: multiply 37 and 24. First, consider 37 as 30 + 7 and 24 as 20 + 4. So our problem becomes (30 + 7) x (20 + 4) or (4 + 20) x (7 + 30) = 4 x (7 + 30) + 20 x (7 + 30). The first multiplication gives the first partial product:: 4 x (7 + 30) = 28 + 120 = 148. The second multiplication gives the second partial product but it is done as: 2(7 + 30) x 10 with the multiplication by 10 done automatically by shifting the product 2(7 + 30) 1 place right. So the second partial product is 14 + 60 = 74(0). The product is obtained by adding the partial products: 148 + 740 = 888.

21. Responses will vary. They may include: 12 x 24 = (10 + 2) x 24 =240+48 = 288;
    12 x 24 = 12 x 25 - 12 = 288. The changes to the original problem produce compatible numbers.

SECTION 4.1

1. 7 is a factor of 87 if 7|87. This test can be carried out several ways: with the INT function on a calculator, by determining if 87 is a multiple of 7 by successive additions, by dividing 87 by 7 and checking for a decimal part of the quotient. This latter division yields 12.43 (to 2 decimal places). Thus 7∤87 and 7 IS NOT a factor of 87.

3. The Factor Test Theorem assures us that the largest number we need to test to determine the factors of 1225 is the square root of 1225, **35**.

5. Divisibility by 2, 3, 4, 5, 6, should be done mentally. The methods are:
    a. Even numbers are divisible by 2. Generally these are recognized by inspection. As a rule, however, the number is divisible by 2 if the right-most digit is divisible by 2.
    b. The rule is: a number is divisible by three is the sum of its digits is divisible by three. Note that this rule can be sequentially applied until a number that is, or is not, divisible by 3 can be determined by inspection. For example: Is 95132695684392 divisible by 3? The sum of its digits is 72. Is 72 divisible by 3? The sum of its digits is 9 which is divisible by 3. So 72 is divisible by 3 as is the original number.
    c. The rule for divisibility by 4 is: if the number formed by the last 2 digits is divisible by 4, then the number is divisible by 4. Recognition of numbers that are multiples of 4 permit this to be done by inspection.
    d. A number is divisible by 5 if the last digit is 0 or 5.
    e. A number is divisible by 6 if it is divisible by 2 and by 3.

7. A large pack of gum contains 15 sticks. Thus to obtain a whole number of large packs of gum with none left over the total number of sticks of gum must be divisible by 15. This could be checked directly. However it may be easier to check divisiblity by 3 and 5 separately. If the total is divisible by both 3 and 5, then it is divisible by 15. We can show this as follows: if N is divisible by 3 and by 5 than N = 3x and N = 5y where x and y are whole numbers. But this means that 3x is divisible by 5 and 5y is divisible by 3. But since 3 does not divide 5 and 5 does not divide 3, then 5 must divide x and 3 must divide y. Thus x = 5a and y = 3b, a and b whole numbers. So N = 15 a = 15 b. Since 15 is a factor of N, 15 divides N. Both 5 and 3 divide 43,860 (last digit 0 and sum of digits, 21, is divisible by 3). Thus a whole number of packages will be produced.

9. Since 7 does not divide 114 (the number formed by the difference between the number formed by all but the last digit and twice the last digit, 11 - 8 = 3, is not divisible by 7) there is not a whole number of 7-day weeks in 114 days.

11. Responses will vary among students. These may include: 28 is a whole number. It is an even number. The factors of 28 are 1,2,4,7,14, and 28. Because the sum of the factors less than 28 sum to 28, it is called a perfect number.

13. Responses will vary among students. Possible answers are determined by applying the following rules.
    To be divisible by 3, the sum of the digits of a number must be a multiple of 3.
    A number divisible by both 2 and 3 is divisible by 6.
    A number is divisible by 9 if the sum of its digits is divisible by 9.
    a. **divisible by 3: 2712**
    b. **divisible by 6: 1716**
    c   **divisible by 9: 6795**

15. a. **True**. 4 | 20 because there is a natural number a, such that 4(a) = 20.   4 x 5 = 20.
    b. **False**. 12 is not a factor of 6 because there is no natural number, n, such that 12 x n = 6.
    c. **True**. 24 | 24 because 24 x 1 = 24.
    d. **False**. 0 ∤ 18 because there is no natural number, n, such that 0 x n = 18.
    e. **False**. 4 does not divide 0 because, although 4 x 0 = 0, 0 is not a natural number. There is no natural number, n, such that 4 x n = 0.
    f. **True**   60 is a multiple of 15 because 15 x 4 = 60.
    g. **False**. 24 is not a divisor of 8 because there is no whole number, n, such that 24 x n = 8.
    h. **False**. Although the relation is true for all natural numbers it is not true for the whole numbers. 0 does not divide 0.

17. a. **True**. Consider the set of non-zero even numbers up to 100 :S={2,4,6,..,96,98,100}. Every other number is a multiple of 4 and thus is divisible by 4. So half of the set is divisible by 4.
    b. **False**. Consider 12. Both 2 and 4 are factors of 12 and thus divide 12 but 8 is not a factor of 12.
    c. **True**. Since 12 divides the number N, then N = 12 x Y, Y some natural number. But N = 6 x (2 x Y). So 6 is a factor of N and 6 divides N.
    d. **False**. Both 4 and 6 divide 12 but 24 is not a factor of 12.

19. a. Because the set of natural numbers is an infinite ordered set, every natural number **always** has an unlimited number of multiples. Suppose that for the natural number N, the largest multiple is Y x M, Y a natural number. But there exists another natural number, Y + 1, larger than Y. And (Y+1) x N is another multiple of N. So Y x N is not the largest multiple of N. So, for any assumed largest multiple of a natural number, we can show that there is yet another, larger, multiple. Thus the number of multiples is unlimited.
    b. This is **sometimes** true. The number 6 has 4 factors: 1, 2, 3, and 6. But 9 has 3 factors: 1, 3, 9.
    c. Except for the situation in which every natural number is a multiple of itself (N = 1 N), this is **never** true. If a is a multiple of b, then a = n(b), n a natural number other than 1. So a > b. But for a to be a factor of b we must have b = n(a), again n a natural number not 1. Thus b > a. But the conditions b > a and a > b cannot both be met unless b = a. But then n has to be one, a situation which we excluded.
    d. Any odd number, o, is a factor of a set of even numbers of the form n x o, n a natural number. Every number had an odd number, 1, as a factor.
    e. If n is a factor of a numbers then the factors of n are **always** factors also. Suppose n is a factor of the natural number a. Then a = n x where x is another factor. Further suppose that y and z are factors of n such that n = y(z). Then a = y(z)(x). Thus y and z are also factors of a.

21. Amicable numbers are numbers such that the sum of the proper factors of each is equal to the other number. Factors of a number may be found by first applying the Factor Test Theorem and then using any of the divisibility test techniques. The proper factors of 220 are: 1, 2 ,4, 5, 10, 11, 20, 22, 44, 55, and 110. The sum of these factors is 284. The proper factors of 284 are 1, 2, 4, 71, and 142. The sum of these factors is 220.

23. Consider:

the number	31	32	33	34	35	36
proper factors	1	1,2,4,8,16	1,3,11	1,2,17	1,5,7	1,2,3,4,6,9,12,18
sum of factors	1	31	15	20	13	55

the number	37	38	39
proper factors	1	1,2,19	1,3,13
sum of factors	1	22	17

In all cases except for 36 the sum of the factors is less than the number. So only 36 is abundant. The other numbers are deficient.

25. Answers will vary. Possible responses include 18 and 36. Since 3, 6, and 9 are some of the factors of 18 (1 and 2 are the other proper factors) and 18 = 3 + 6 + 9, 18 is a semi-perfect number. The proper factors of 36 are 1, 2, 3, 4, 6, 9, 12, and 18. The sum (3+6+9+18) = 36. So 36 is another semi-perfect number.

27. Let N be the number we are seeking. If N divided by seven leaves a remainder of 0, then N must be a multiple of 7. When N is divided by 2, 3, 4, and 5 the remainder is 1. Thus 2, 3, 4, 5 are factors of N - 1. Since a number with a factor of 4 also has a factor if 2, N - 1 is a multiple of $3 \cdot 4 \cdot 5 = 60$. The smallest such multiple is 60 itself. So N itself is a (multiple of 60) + 1 that is divisible by 7. Multiples of 60, plus 1, are 61, 121, 181, 241, 301, ... Now, 301 divided by 7 = 43, so 301 is a solution. Trial shows that others are 721, 1141, and 1561. Note that 301=5(60)+1, 721=12(60)+1, 1141=19(60)+1, and 1561=26(60)+1. This pattern suggests that the solutions are of the form N = (5 + 7n) 60 + 1, n = 0, 1, 2, 3, 4, ...

29. a. Begin by adding the factors from largest to smallest, checking the sum after each addition. The sum of 78 and 52 is 130. The sum of 130 and 39, 169, is greater than 156. So 156 is abundant.
    b. Janie might apply some estimation techniques. Replace all the factors with the next higher number of 10's: 10, 10, 20, 30, 40, 100. The sum of these, which is an overestimate of the exact sum, is seen to be 210, less than 273. Thus 273 is deficient.

31. Responses will vary. Possible responses include: 4|32. But 32 can be expressed as (20+12) and 4|12. So we have a situation in which n|(a+b) and n|b. But 4|20. So we also have n|a. Thus 4|(12+20) is an example of a situation in which since n|(a+b) and n|b, n|a.

33. Suppose M is the mother's age, D the daughter's. The condition that dividing the ages by 2 leaves a remainder of 1 means that the ages of both mother and daughter are odd numbers. So far, then the ages are in the set {1,3,5,7,9,11,13,15,17,19,21,23,25,27,29,31,33,35,37,39,41,...}. The condition that division by 3 leave a remainder of 2 ensures that the ages are in the set {2,5,8,11,14,17,20,23,26,29,32,35,38,...} and the condition that division by 4 leaves a remainder of 3 places the ages in the set {3,7,11,15,19,23,27,31,35,39,43,...}. The intersection of these 3 sets is {11,23,35,47,59,71,...}. Finally applying the condition that M is about 3D, we can conclude that **D = 11 and M = 35**.

35. Responses will vary. One argument is: since 43 is not divisible by 3, and since the scoring supposedly happened in 3's or in multiples of 3's, the score of 43 is not possible. No whole number multiple of 3 is 43. 14 times 3 is 42 and 15 times 3 is 45.

37. Solutions will vary. One possible solution is: we know that 24 notebooks were purchased, the cost per notebook was between $2.00 and $3.00, and the product of the number and cost is $_7.3_. If we do our computations on a calculator in pennies, the minimum cost of a notebook is 201, the number is 24, the total cost is 4824 pennies. This is not the correct price because the middle digits are not 73. Now, we use the keystroke sequence +,24,=,=,=,=,... to produce multiples of 24 until the display shows a number with 73 as the middle digits. As each = is pressed count: "202, 203, 204,..." The display shows 5736 on the count of "239'. The cost of one notebook is **$2.39**.

39. The proper factors of 120 are: 1,2,3,4,5,6,8,10,12,15,20,24,30,40,60. The sum of these is 240, 2 times 120. The proper factors of 672 are: 1,2,3,4,6,7,8,12,14,16,21,24,28,32,42,48,56,84,96,112,168,224,336. The sum of these numbers is 1344 which is 2 times 672.

SECTION 4.2

1. By definition a prime number has 2 and only 2 distinct factors, 1 and the number itself.

3. A composite number has at least 3 distinct factors.

5. a. Since 8 may be expressed as the product of more than 2 factors, $8 = 1 \times 2 \times 4$, **8 is composite**.
   b. Since 11 may only be expressed as the product of 1 and 11, 2 factors, **11 is prime**.
   c. Because 1 cannot be expressed as the product of two or more unique factors, 1 is **neither prime nor composite.**
   d. Since 51 can be expressed as the product of 3 and 17, **51 is composite**.
   e. Since 221 can be expressed as $1 \times 13 \times 17$, **221 is composite**.

7.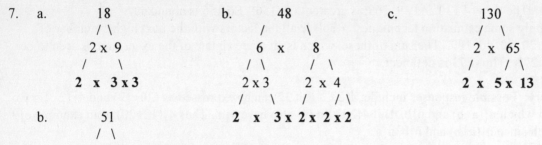

   3 x 17 The order of the factors may vary among student responses.

9. The **8** pairs of twin primes are: **3-5, 5-7, 11-13, 17-19, 29-31, 41-43, 59-61, 71-73.**

11. $16,731 \div 3 = 5577$, $5577 \div 3 = 1859$, $1859 \div 11 = 169$, $169 = 13 \times 13$. So $16,731 = $ **3x3x11x13x13**.

13. a. $888 \div 259 = 3$ R 111; $259 \div 111 = 2$ R 37; $111 \div 37 = 3$ R 0. So GCF = **37**.
    b. $308 \div 84 = 3$ R 56; $84 \div 56 = 1$ R 28; $56 \div 28 = 2$ R 0. GCF = **28**.
    c. $7560 \div 1232 = 6$ R 168; $1232 \div 168 = 7$ R 56; $168 \div 56 = 3$ R 0. GCF = **56**.

15. Apply the GCF-LCM Theorem: the product of the GCF and LCM of two numbers is equal to the product of the two numbers. So $36 \times$ GCF = 108. Thus the GCF is **3**.

17. Since the small plots are to be squares the lengths and widths of all the small plots must be equal. Call this length L. Thus L must divide evenly into both the length and width of the large plot. Since we want the largest small plots, we want L to be the GCF of 70 and 525. Applying the Euclidian Algorithm: $525 \div 70 = 7$ R 35; $70 \div 35 = 2$ R 0. Thus the GCF is 35 and the small plots should be **35 feet by 35 feet**.

19. If the formula is written as $p = n^2 + (-n + 41)$ it is easily seen that when 41 is substituted for n, the expression in the parentheses has a value of 0 and $p = n^2$.   So p is not only the product of 1 and p but also the product of 1, n and n. Since p can be written as the product of more than 2 factors it is not prime.

21. The first 4 primes are 2, 3, 5, and 7. The values of $2^p - 1$ are, respectively, 3, 7, 31, 127, all primes. But $2^{11} - 1 = 2047$. The product of 1, 89, and 23 equals 2047. Thus 2047 is not prime.

23.

	x	x	x	x	x
xx	x	x	xx	11	xx
13	xx	xx	xx	17	xx
19	xx	xx	xx	23	xx
xx	xx	xx	xx	29	xx
31	xx	xx	xx	xx	xx
37	xx	xx	xx	41	xx
43	xx	xx	xx	47	xx
xx	xx	xx	xx	53	xx
xx	xx	xx	xx	59	xx
61	xx	xx	xx	xx	xx
67	xx	xx	xx	71	xx
73	xx	xx	xx	xx	xx
79	xx	xx	xx	83	xx
xx	xx	xx	xx	89	xx
xx	xx	xx	xx	xx	xx
97	xx	xx	xxx		

Responses will vary. All responses should include the observation that primes are only in columns 1 and 5 and primes have the form $6n + 1$ or $6n - 1$. Some other patterns are: numbers divisible by 3 are in columns 3 and 6; multiples of 5 are on diagonals with higher positions left; multiples of 7 are on diagonals in the opposite direction.

25. Testing 5773 for divisibility by numbers no greater than the square root, 75, we find that $5773 = 23 \times 251$. Thus 5773 is **not** prime.

27. The greatest common factor of a pair of numbers is always less than the least common multiple. The LCM can be bo smaller than the larger of the 2 numbers. The GCF can be no larger than the smaller of the 2 numbers, For example, consider the numbers 15 and 35. The **LCM**, by definition of multiple, **must be divisible by** both 15 and 35. Since $15 = 3 \times 5$ and $35 = 5 \times 7$, the LCM is $3 \times 5 \times 7 = 105$. But the **GCF must divide into** each of the numbers. The GCF is 5.

29. a. 6 is a prime in E because it has no divisors in E other that 1 and 6.
   b. The first 5 primes in E are: **2, 6, 10, 14, 18.**
   c. The primes appear to have the form $p = 4n + 2$, n a whole number.
   d. The composites appear to have the form $c = 4n$, n a natural number.
   e. The formula does generate the primes in E. Examples: $2(2) - 2 = 2$; $2(4) - 2 = 6$, and so on.
   f. Since the set E is infinite and there are infinitely many numbers in E of the form $2 + 4n$, n a whole number, **the number of primes in E is infinite**.
   g. One formula is given in d, another is $c = 2 \times e$ where e is an element of E greater than 1
   h. Except for $e = 1$, in which case $2 \times e = 2$, a prime, 2 times an element in e is not prime because such a number has at least 3 factors in E, 1, 2, and e.
   i. In the set of natural numbers, twin primes are primes that differ by only 2, such as 3 and 5. Now, with this criterion there are no twin primes in E because the minimum difference between any two primes is 4. However, if twin primes are primes separated by one composite, the there are an infinite number of pairs of twin primes in E because in E primes alternate with composites.
   j. Goldbach's Conjecture is: "Every even number greater than 2 is the sum of 2 primes.". 6 is a counterexample to the conjecture in E. 6, in E, is $2 + 4$ but 4 is a composite. Examination of the composites, however, $8 = 2 + 6$, $12 = 2 + 10$, $16 = 6 + 10$, suggests the conjecture that "Every composite in E can be represented as sum of 2 primes."

31. All even numbers greater than 2 are divisible by 2. Thus 2 is a factor. But primes have only 1 and the number as factors. Thus an even number greater than 2 cannot be a prime.

33. Responses will vary. A possible argument is: a square number, S, can be represented as the product of 2 identical factors: S = (s)(s). Thus s is a factor of S in addition to 1 and S. Thus S has at least 3 distinct factors and cannot be prime.

35.

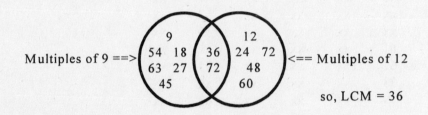

$$\text{Multiples of 9} ==> \begin{array}{c} 9 \\ 54 \quad 18 \\ 63 \quad 27 \\ 45 \end{array} \begin{array}{c} 36 \\ 72 \end{array} \begin{array}{c} 12 \\ 24 \quad 72 \\ 48 \\ 60 \end{array} <== \text{Multiples of 12}$$

so, LCM = 36

37. $24 \div 2 = 12$; $12 \div 2 = 6$. $6 \div 2 = 3$. $2\not/3$. So the exponent of 2 is 3. Finally, $3 \div 3 = 1$. So $24 = 2^3 \times 3^1$; The exponents are 3 and 1. The increased exponents are 4 and 2 and their product is 8. Now, the factors of 24 are 1, 2, 3, 4, 6, 8, 12, 24. There are 8 factors.

39. Responses will vary. A possible solution is: let C = the cost of 1 watch and N the number of watches. We know that C and N are both natural numbers, C > N, and C x N = 437. Now, pairs of factors of 437 are: 1 and 437, 19 and 23. Since we know that there were 'several' watches, he must have ordered **19 watches** at **$23 each**.

41. Various approaches are possible. One is: Because the ones digit is prime, the initial set of possibilities for the ones digit is {2,3,5,7}. The hundreds digit is also prime. So the possibilities for the hundreds digit are the set {2, 3, 5, or 7}. Because the number formed by the hundreds and tens digits is prime, the number formed by the left and middle digits is in the set S = {23, 29, 31, 37, 53, 59, 73, 79}. Because the entire 3 digit number is prime, neither 2 nor 5 is a possibility for the ones digit. So, considering the entire set of possibilities in which the hundred-ten digits are from S and the ones digit is either 3 or 7, we have as possibilities (and the reasons for eliminating them) : eliminated because not all digits are different: 233, 313, 373, 377, 533, 733, 737, and eliminated because not prime: 237 = (3)(79), 537 = (3)(179), 297=(3)(99). Eliminated because they are not area codes: 293 and 593. We are left with **317, Indiana**.

43. Responses will vary. One algorithm is: determine the integer part of the square root (m) of the number (N). Sequentially test the natural numbers from 2 the integer part of the square root for divisibility. If one of these numbers is found to be divisible then the number is not prime. If none of these numbers is divisible then the number is prime.

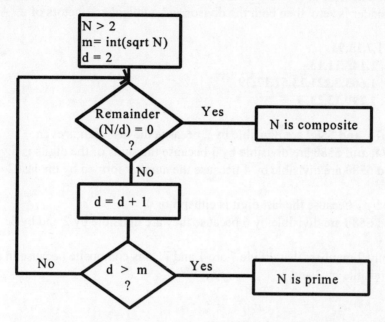

45. Responses will vary among students. One such program is: INPUT X, INPUT Y, IF X < Y, GOTO 1, X-->A, Y-->B, GOTO 2, LBL 1, X-->B, Y-->A, LBL 2, REMAINDER(A,B)-->R, IF R=0, GOTO 3, B-->A, R-->B, GOTO 2, LBL 3, DISP "GCF OF", DISP X, DISP Y, DISP 'IS', DISP B

47. Responses will vary among students. They may discuss the relations in terms of set as: even and odd numbers are disjoint subsets of the whole numbers. The intersection of the set of prime numbers and the even numbers is the set {2}. The set of composite numbers has elements in both the set of evens and in the set of odds. No square numbers are in the set of primes.

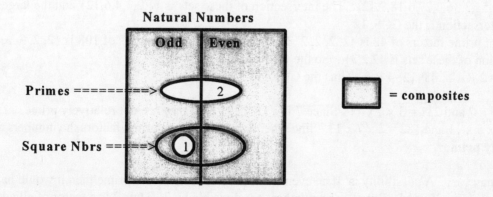

CHAPTER 4 REVIEW EXERCISES

1. To determine the factors of a number n, divide n by the natural numbers less than or equal to the square root of the number. If the remainder is zero, then both the divisor and quotient are factors of n. Applying this strategy we get:
   a. The factors of 18 are: **1, 18, 2, 9, 3, 6.**
   k. The factors of 32 are: **1,32,2,16,4,8.**

l.   The factors of 48 are: **1,48,2,24,3,16,4,12,6,8**.

m.   The factors of 105 are: **1,105, 3,35,5,21,7,15**.

3.   To determine the factors of a number n, divide n by the natural numbers less than or equal to the square root of the number. If the remainder is zero, then both the divisor and quotient are factors of n. Applying this strategy we get:

a.   The factors of 91 are: **1,7,13,91**.

b.   The factors of 143 are: **1,143,11,13**.

c.   The factors of 663 are: **1,663,3,221,13,51,17,39**.

d.   The factors of 299 are: **1,299,13,23**.

5.   a.   The numbers **1436, 4674, and 5580** are divisible by 2 becasue the last digit is even.

b.   The numbers **987, 4674, and 5580** are divisible by 3 because the sums of the digits is divisible by 3.

c.   The numbers **1436 and 5580** are divisible by 4 because the number formed by the last 2 digits is divisible by 4.

d.   Only **5580** is divisible by 5 because the last digit is either 5 or 0.

e.   The numbers **4674 and 5580** are divisible by 6 because they are divisible by 2 and by 3.

7.   7 is a prime because the only 2 numbers that divide 7 are 1 and 7. 6 is composite because in addition to being divisible by 1 and 6 it is divisible by 2 and 3.

9.   a.
```
         90                    420
       2 x 45                2 x 210
     2 x 3 x 15            2 x 5 x 42
   2 x 3 x 3 x 5         2 x 5 x 2 x 21
                       2 x 5 x 2 x 3 x 7
```

b.   90÷2=45; 45÷3=15; 15÷3=**5**.   420÷2=210; 210÷5=42; 42÷2=21; 21÷3=**7**.

11. a.   The set of factors of 48 is {1,48,2, 24,3,16,4,12, 6,8} The set of factors of 108 is {1,108,2,54,3,36,4,27,6,18,9,12}. The intersection of these sets is {1,2,3,4,6,12} and the largest element of the intersection is the GCF, **12**

b.   The set of prime factors of 48 is {2, 2, 2, 2 ,3} and the set of prime factors of 108 is {2, 2, 3, 3, 3,}. The intersection of these sets is {2,2,3} . So the GCF is 2 x 2 x 3 = **12**.

c.   108÷48= 2 R 12. 48÷12=4 R 0. Thus the GCF is **12**.

13. a.   70 = 2 x 5 x 7 and 231 = 3 x 7 x 11. Since 7 is a factor of both they are not relatively prime.

b.   165 = 3 x 5 x 11 and 182 = 2 x 7 x 13. Since there are no common prime factors the numbers are **relatively prime**.

15. Arguments may vary. A possibility is: If an even number other than 2 were prime then it would have no factors other than itself and 1. But all even numbers are divisible by 2. Thus 2 is a factor of all even numbers. So no even number other than 2 is prime.

17. Arguments will vary. A possible argument is: In N is to be divisible by 2, 3, 4, 5, 6, and 7, each of these must be factors of N. But if 6 is a factor of N, so are 2 and 3. So keep 2 and 3 and drop 6. Similarly, since 4 is a factor, so is 2. So keep 4 and drop 2. So we have as factors 3,4,5, and 7. The product of these is **420**.

19. a. We must find the LCM of 90 and 240, convert this time to hours, and add that number of hours to 12:00 noon. 90 = 2 x 3 x 3 x 5. 240 = 2 x 2 x 2 x 2 x 3 x 5. So the LCM is 2 x 2 x 2 x 2 x 3 x 3 x 5 = 720 min. 720 min = 12 hours. The sirens will sound simultaneously at midnight.

   b. Since 720÷90 = 8. So A will sound again 8 times for a total of 9. And B will sound (720÷240) + 1, 4 times.

21. a. The square plots must have both length and width equal to the GCF of 560 and 528. The prime factorizations are: 560 = 2 x 2 x 2 x 2 x 5 x 7. and 528 - 2 x 2 x 2 x 2 x 3 x 11. The GCF = 16. The largest research plots are **16 m x 16 m.**

   b. The total area divided by the area of a research plot [(560 x 528)÷(16 x 16)] = **1155**.

   c. Smaller plots could have and edge length that is a factor of 16: 1, 2, 4, or 8.

23. Responses depend upon group interactions of the students.

SECTION 5.1

1. a   The number of points is a positive integer. The process of losing is negative. So "Lose 5 points." is
        represented **-5**. The opposite situation is **to gain 5 points** represented by **5**.
    b. Six seconds before blastoff is a negative integer and is represented ⁻**6** seconds. The opposite situation is
        six seconds after blastoff represented by **6** seconds.
    c. The amount of money is represented by a positive integer and the process of making a profit is positive.
        So a profit of $8500 is represented as **8500** dollars. The opposite situation is **to lose $8500** represented by
        -8500 dollars.

3. In the following O = 1, X = -1.
    a. OOO   X   OX OO   OO   b.   XXX   OO   XO XO   X   X
        OOO + X = OX OO = OO   XX + O = XO   X = X
        OO   X   OX O   O   XX   O   XO   X   X
             8 + (-3) = 5   -7 + 4 = -3

    c. XX   OO   XO XO
        XX + OO =   XO XO = X
        X   X
             -5 + 4 = -1

5. Responses will vary. Possible responses are:
    a. 11 is represented by a set of 11 black chips. The opposite of 5 is represented by a set of 5 red chips. The
        union of the two sets is formed and each red chip is paired with a black chip. There are 6 unpaired black
        chips. Thus the sum of 11 and -5 is 6.
    b. Begin at 0 on the number line and move 7 units to the left to represent the opposite of 7. Then move 9
        units to the right to represent the addition of 9. The final position on the number line is 2. So -7 + 9 = 2.
    c. Form the union between a set of 6 red chips and a set of 8 black chips. Pair red and black chips and count
        the unpaired chips. Since there are 2 unpaired black chips, the result of adding the opposite of 6 to 8 is 2.

7. a. Associative property of addition: (5 + 4) + -4 = 5 + (4 + -4)
    b. Additive inverse property: (4 + -4) = 0
    c. Additive identity property: 5 + 0 = 5.

9. a. -7 - (-8) = -7 + [-(-8)]. But -(-8) is the opposite of - 8 which is 8. So -7 + [-(-8)] =-7 + 8 = 1.
    b. -9 -5 = -9 +(-5) = -14.
    c. 11 - (-4) = 11 +[-(-4)]. As in a, [-(-4)], the opposite of -4, is 4. So 11 +[-(-4)] 11 + 4 = 15.

11. a. -6 -9 = **-15**.   b. -15 - (-6) = -15 + 6 = **-9**.   c. -6 - (-6) = -6 + 6 = **0**.   d. -6 + (-6) = **-12**.

13. Conceptually, LOSS + GAIN = NET. Losses are represented by negative integers and gains by positive
     integers. So the decrease in the price of the stock is represented by LOSS = ⁻5, the increase by GAIN = 9. So
     we have ⁻**5 + 9 = NET**. So the NET or TOTAL GAIN for the 2 days is **$4**.

15. a. The order, largest to smallest, is: **21, 8, 0, -4, -6, -9, -12, -15.**
     b. The order, largest to smallest, is: **23, 18, 17, 9, -2, -12, -15, -18.**
     c. The order, largest to smallest, is: **-13,570, -13,999, -14,000.**

17. On the conventional number line larger numbers are to the right of smaller numbers.

Since -13 is to the right of -19 we have -13 > -19.

19. To solve the equation a - (-459) = 9236, first change it to the equivalent equation a + 459 = 9236. So a = 9236 - 459 = **$8777**.

21. Approaches and calculator key sequences will vary. Possibilities include:
   a. The key sequence: 789, +, 564, =, +/- gives **-1353**
   b. The key sequence: 4986, -, (, -, 5278,), = gives **10264**.
   c. The key sequence: -, 876, +, 1269, = gives **393**.
   d. The key sequence: 9876, -, 7864, = gives **2012**.

23. a. The pattern could be generated by successive additions of 4. So the pattern might be ⁻8, ⁻4, 0, **4, 8, 12**.
   b. The pattern could be generated by successive subtractions of 7: 15, 8, 1, ⁻**6, ⁻13, ⁻20**.
   c. One way to generate the first 3 numbers after 5 is to subtract 15, add 20, subtract 30. Continuing the pattern by add 40, subtract 50, add 60 we get: -20 + 40 = 20, 20 - 50 = -30, -30 + 60 = 30. So the sequence becomes: 5, -10, 10, -20, **20, -30, 30**.
   d. The first 5 numbers in the pattern could be generated by beginning with 1 then successively adding ⁻3, 4, ⁻5, 6, ... to each successive number. Doing this produces: 1, 1+⁻3=⁻2, ⁻2+4=2, 2+⁻5=⁻3, ⁻3+6=3, 3+⁻7=⁻**4**, ⁻**4+8=4**, 4+⁻9=⁻**5**.

25. a. A week from now would be represented by the positive integer **7**.
   b. Yesterday would be represented by the negative integer ⁻**1**.
   c. A week ago would be represented by ⁻**7**.
   d. The day after tomorrow would be represented by 1 + 1 = **2**.
   e. A month from now could be represented by **30**.

27. The additive inverse of an integer is another integer such that the sum of the 2 integers is 0
   a. ⁻k + **k** = 0.   b. (j + k) + ⁻**(j + k)** = 0.   c. j + ⁻**j** = 0.   d. (j - k) + ⁻**(j - k)** = 0 = **-j+k**.

29. Responses will vary. A possibility is: a drop in temperature will be represented by a negative integer. Now, the beginning temperature, B, plus the drop, D, is equal to the ending temperature, E. So B + D = E. Substituting the given values, 5 + D = ⁻3. So D = ⁻**8**.

31. Methods of solution will vary. Possibilities include:
   a. Since 1 must be added to -6 to get -5, **x = 1**.
   b. Adding 4 to -9 we find that **n = -5**.
   c. Adding 8 to 12 we find that **y = 20**.
   d. Subtracting - 4 from -4+12, we find z = -4 + 12 - (-4) = **12**.
   e. Since t - (-9) = 2 is equivalent to t + 9 = 2 we can add -9 to each side of the equation. So **t = -7**.
   f. Subtracting -4 from 7 + -4 gives 7 + (-4) - (-4) = r. So **r = 7**.

33.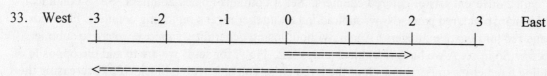

The final position of the car is three miles west of the station.

35. One might begin this exercise by ordering the numbers: -61, -49, -29, -21, 39, 45, 56.
    a.   **-49 + 45** = -4.
    b.   **-61 + (-49)** = -110.
    c.   **39 + 56** = 95.
    d.   **39 - (-61)** = 100.
    e.   **-21 - (-29)** = 8.
    f.   **39 - 45**= -6.

37.   Estimates and methods will vary. Possibilities include:
    a.   Estimate by **rounding**: 700 - 500 = **200**.
    b.   All of the values **cluster** around -500. So -500 - 500 - 500 - 500 - 500 = 5(-500) = **-2500**.
    c.   Using **compatible numbers** and **breaking apart** the result is approximated by:
         -300-50 + 50 + 1200 = **900**.
    d.   **Front-end estimation** gives the approximation -800,000 + 300,000 = **-500,000**.
    e.   **Rounding** to estimate gives -400 -800 +200 + 1000 - 700 = **-700**.

39.   To complete the magic square first find the missing addend in the diagonal (7) the missing addend in row 2, and so on. The square is:
```
-2   3  -7   4
 0  -3   7  -6
 5  -8   2  -1
-5   6  -4   1
```

41.   Using the numbers -3, -2, -1, 0, 1, 2, 3 the following triplets sum to 2: (-3, 3, 2), (-2, 3, 1), (-1, 1, 2), (-1, 0, 3).
      These can be arranged in a triangle the following ways so that each side has a sum of 2:
```
        1                      3
     -2   2                 -3   0
    3   0  -1              2   1  -1
```

43.   The story will vary among students. The facts are: The home team scored on its first possession with **80** net yards of offense. After a successful conversion the home team led 7 - 0. The visitors received the ball on the kickoff and returned it 24 yards. On their first possession the visitors punted after a net gain of 6 yards. The visitors netted **30** yards including the kick-off return.

45.   After 2 rounds Drivefar is 3 strokes above Puttgood. Puttgood picks up an additional 7 strokes on 7 holes. So with 11 holes yet to be scored, Puttgood is 10 strokes ahead of Drivefar. But Drivefar can gain 1 stroke on each of the eleven holes. He has the potential to win by 1 stroke.

47.   Responses will vary. One possibility is: the arrow model is similar to the colored counter model in that there are a variety of representations of any integer because an opposite pair, red/black counters or left/right arrows represent 0. So as 6 could be represented by 6 black counters or 8 black and 2 red or 10 black and 4 red it could also be represented by 6 unit arrows to the right or 8 arrows to the right and 2 to the left or 10 to the right and 4 to the left.

49.   Responses will vary. A possibility is: Use the chip model. Represent some integer, i, say positive without losing generality, with 2 different sets of colored counters. Set A contains i black counters. Set B contains i black counters and b more black/red pairs. Now, subtracting an integer means removing counters, black for positive integers and red for negative integers. Again, without losing generality, suppose we are to subtract the positive number b. So in set A we have (i-b) black chips left. Now, for set B we are to add the opposite of b. This means adding b red chips to B. But each of the b red chips can pair with b black chips decreasing the

net number of unpaired black chips by b. So both sets A and B have the same number of unpaired black chips and thus represent the same number.

51. **Yes**, the method is correct. We know that -7 + 4 = -3. Now let's add the following procedure. Since these integers are of unlike sign we first determine the absolute values of the integers and subtract the lesser from the greater. This gives us 7 - 4 = 3. Now, since -7 has the greater absolute value we append the sign '-' to the 3 resulting in -3. Secondly, we know that -3 + (-2) is -5. Following the procedure, we would add the absolute values and give the sum the sign of the integers, - in this case. So we have 3 + 2 = 5 and, with the sign, -5.

53. Responses will vary. A possibility is: a slash through a group of vertical tally marks anywhere within the numeral indicates that the number is negative. The numeration system is place value based on powers of 10. The initial tally may be either horizontal or vertical. Tallying continues through 5 within a place. After that a single line, horizontal if tallying was done with vertical lines, vertical if tallying was done with horizontal lines. is used to represent 5. This line is not added until the face value becomes 6.

SECTION 5.2

1. a. $0(-5) = $ **0**   b. $-1(-5) = $ **5**   c. $-2(-5) = $ **10**   d. $-3(-5) = $ **15**

3. Responses will vary. Possible responses include:
    a. Begin at 0 on the number line. Walk 7 units to the left 9 consecutive times. Your final position is **-63**.
    b. Apply the rule that the product of 2 negatives is positive and use a calculator to find the product of 894 and 567, the product $-894(-567) = $ **506,898**.
    c. Do the opposite of placing 10 groups of 8 counters in a bag, that is, take 10 groups of 8 counters out of a bag. The number of counters in the bag has decreased by 80. So, $-10(8) = $ **-80**.

5. a. $-56 = 8 \times ?.\ ? = $ **-7**.   b. $-48 = -6 \times ?.\ ? = $ **8**.   c. $36 = -9 \times ?.\ ? = $ **-4**.

7. Let T represent the total change. Then $T = 5(-\$4) = $ **-\$20**.

9. a. $95(-46) = $ **-4370**   b. $-180(47) = $ **-8460**   c. $-34(-67) = $ **2278**

11. Responses will vary. Possibilities include: One might multiply 3 by 27 (obtaining 81) and add the knowledge that the product of 2 negatives is a positive as a justification. Or one might use the interpretation of division as repeated subtraction, repeatedly subtracting 27 from a beginning number of 81 until 0 is reached, counting the number of subtractions and then adjust for sign..

13. Subtracting 12 from 0 ten consecutive times demonstrates the calculation **$10(-12) = $ - 120** .

15. Responses will vary. Possibilities include:
    a. $-2(-y) = 2y$: For all pairs of integers a and b, $(-a)(-b) = ab$ by the property of opposites.
    b. Since $-(2x - 4) = (-1)(2x - 4)$ and $(-1)(2x - 4) = (-1)(2x) - (-1)(4)$ by the distributive property and $(-1)(2x) - (-1)(4) = -2x + 4$ by the property of opposites, we have $-(2x - 4) = -2x + 4$.
    c. $-1(ab) = -(ab)$ by the property of opposites..

17. Positive integer exponents represent the number of times a number is to be used as a factor in multiplication
    a. $5^3 = 5 \times 5 \times 5 = $ **125**.   b. $(-2)^2 = (-2) \times (-2) = $ **4**   c. $(-5)^3 = (-5)(-5)(-5) = $ **-125**
    d. $(-3)^4 \div (-3)^3 = (-3)(-3)(-3)(-3)/(-3)(-3)(-3) = $ **-3**

19.

X	Pos	Neg	0
Pos	Pos	Neg	0
Neg	Neg	Pos	0
0	0	0	0

21. a. A possible pattern is based on successive additions of -6, 8, -12, 14, -18, 20, -24, 26, ... The absolute values of the additions alternate between 2 and 4 and the signs alternate. So, beginning with 2, we have the pattern: 2, (2-6=-4), (-4+8=4), (4-12=-8), (-8+14=6), (6-18=-12), (-12+20=8), (8-24=-16), (-16+26=**10**), (10-30=**-20**), (-20+32=**12**).

   b. A possibility is a sequence beginning with 1 and each succeeding term is obtained by multiplying by -2. This produces: 1, -2, 4, -8, 16, -32, **64, -128, 256.**

   c. A possibility for this pattern is successive multiplications by -3. 2, -6, 18, -54, 162, **-486, 1458, -4374**.

   d. A possibility is to successively add numbers which have absolute values that are determined by multiplying 7 by successive powers of 2 and then appending alternating signs to get the successive addends beginning with a -. So the addends are -7, 14, -28, 56, -112, 224, - 448, 896. So, successively adding these numbers to each term beginning with 2 we get: 2, -5, 9, -19, 37, -75, **149, -299, 597.**

23. Responses will vary. A possible argument is: -a is, by definition, the opposite of a. Thus -a + a = 0. Now consider the expression [a(-1) + a]: a(-1) + a = a(-1) + a(1) [multiplicative identity] = a (-1 + 1) [distributive property] = a (0) [definition of additive inverse] = 0 [zero property]. Thus both -a and a(-1) are additive inverses of a. But the additive inverse of an integer is unique. So -a = a(-1).

25. Responses will vary. Possibilities include: a ÷ b = c iff there is a unique integer, c, such that a = b x c. Now, if 0 ÷ 0 = 5 is correct, then 0 = 0 x 5 only for the integer 5. But 0 times any integer = 0. So 5 is not unique in the expression 0 = 0 x 5. Thus the division 0 ÷ 0 is not defined.

27. Responses will vary. Student responses may include: Whereas integer multiplication is associative, integer division is not: (24 x 6) x 2 = 24 x (6 x 2) = 288 but (24÷6)÷2 = 2 but 24÷(6÷2) = 8. Multiplication is commutative, division is not. 12 x 2 = 2 x 12 but 12÷2 is not equal to 2÷12.

29. Responses may vary. Possibilities include:
   a. Additive identity.
   b. Distributive property.
   c. Additive identity.
   d. The additive identity element in the set of integers is a unique element. Since both 0 and a· 0 add to a · 1 to yield a · 1, they must be different representations of the same element and thus be equal.

31. The total of the overages and underages is: 8(-3) + 6(-5) + 9(4) + 2(-7) = -32. So the total weight is 32 lb under 25(50). Total = 25(50) - 32 = **1218 lbs**.

33. Responses will vary. A possible response is: Negative integers represent bills, positive integers represent cash. Cash is necessary to pay bills. More cash is required to pay 'bigger' bills than is required to pay 'smaller' bills. When one says that a $50 bill is larger than a $25 bill that person is actually referring to the cash required to pay the bill, not suggesting that -50 is a larger number than -25. The absolute value of -50 is greater than the absolute value of -25 but -50 itself is less than -25.

35. Responses will vary. One possibility is: A Korean mathematician may have formed a set from the union of 4 sets of 3 black rods. Counting the number of rods in this set he arrived at 12 black rods which is represented as -12.

37. The responses to this question depend upon group interactions among students. In their discussions they may address the following: multiplication can be performed by repeated addition and division by repeated subtraction. Multiplication and addition are commutative and associative but subtraction and division are neither. The integers are closed under addition, multiplication and subtraction but not under division. Multiplication and division with operands of the same sign produce positive results.

CHAPTER 5 REVIEW EXERCISES

1. a. **True.**
    b. **False. The sum of a positive and a negative integer may be positive, negative, or 0.**
    c. **False.** The absolute value of 0 is 0 and 0 is not positive.
    d. **False. The product of 2 negative integers is always positive.**
    e. **False. The integer 0 is neither positive nor negative.**

3. a. **-7**   b. **-4**   c. **-8**   d. **9**

5. a. The number 2 can be represented by a set of counters in which there are 2 more black that red. So represent 2 with 10 black and 8 red counters. The process of subtraction is represented physically by removing counters, black for positive numbers, red for negative. So remove 5 red counters. We are left with a set with 10 black and 3 red counters This set represents the number 7.
    b. Begin at the position on the number line that represents 2. Now, do the opposite (the subtraction sign) of moving left 5 units (the number -5). So move right 5 units. The final position, 7, represents 2 - (-5).
    c. The opposite of -5 is 5. Executing subtraction by adding the opposite, then, yields 2 + 5 = 7.

7. The larger of 2 integers is farther to the right on a number line.

9. a. Since the second factor is -4 we are moving sets of 4 red counters. Because the absolute value of the first factor is 3 we are moving 3 sets of 4 red counters. Since the sign of the first factor is negative we will remove 3 sets of 4 red counters from a set that originally contained equal numbers of red and black counters. This set now contains 12 more black than red counters. So the product is 12.
    b. On the number line we will do the opposite of moving left 4 spaces 3 times beginning at 0. This means that we will move right 4 units 3 times. The final position is 12.
    c. 3(-4) = -12,   2(-4) = -8,   1(-4) = -4,   0(-4) = 0   -1(-4) = 4   -2(-4) = 8   -3(-4) = 12.

11. a. Distributive property of multiplication over addition..
    b. Associative property of multiplication.
    c. Additive inverse property.
    d. Distributive property.
    e. For all non-zero integers b, b÷b = 1.
    f. The associative property of multiplication and theproperty of opposites.

13. Order the months:
    a. Nov Dec Jan Feb Mar Apr May Jun July Aug Sep Oct Nov Dec
               -5   -4   -3   -2   -1   0   1   2   3   4   5   6
        Jan = -5, Mar = -3, May = -1, Aug = 2, Oct = 4, Dec = 6.
    b. Counting to count backwards on the above diagram, -7 is associated with **November**.

15. Responses may vary. Possibilities include:
    a. Associative property of addition..
    b. Additive inverse property.
    c. Additive identity property.

17. Let H represent the record high temperature and let L represent the record low. H - L = 192. Also H -4 = -L. So we have, from the first equation, H = 192 + L. Thus 192 + L - 4 = -L; 188 + L = -L; 2L = -188; **L = -94**. From the first relation, H = 192 + L = 192 + (-94) = **98**.

19. Responses will vary. The facts are that the test showed that the sample of 50 bags was a total of 53 oz light. This is about 1 oz per bag. A bag is sold at a weight of 50 lb, 800 oz. Essentially, the company is getting the income for 800 bags when selling 799 bags worth of fertilizer.

21. The tables are:

+	P	N
P	P	S
N	S	N

-	P	N
P	S	P
N	N	S

x	P	N
P	P	N
N	N	P

÷	P	N
P	P	N
N	N	P

The discussion of the value and limitations will vary among students. Responses may include the ideas that the tables are valuable as summary devices but are limited by the S entries.

SECTION 6.1

1.   Models may vary. Possibilities include:

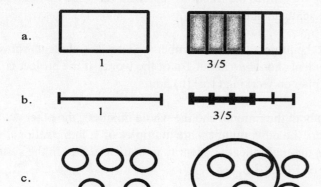

3.   Letting the hundreds square represent 1, the thousands cube represents 10 because 10 hundreds equals 1000.
      The tens stick represents 0.1 because 1/10 of a hundred is 10. Finally, the units cube represents 0.01 because
      1/100 of one hundred is 1.

5.   a. $4 \times \frac{1}{2} = 2$ b. $-18 \times -1/18 = 1$ c. $\frac{1}{2} \times 6 = 3$ d. $386/1000 \times 1000 = 386$

7.   Fraction form   Decimal form
      a.   160/25   **6.4**
      b.   **386/1000**   0.386
      c.   **2/3**   0.666....
      d.   4/11   **0.3636...**

9.   Responses will vary. Different calculators have different scientific notation displays. Possibilities include:
      a. **3.48   09 or 3.48 E9**   b. **9.08   -05 or 9.08 E-5**   c. **6.085   00 or 6.085**

11.

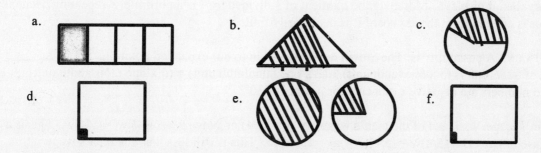

13.   Explanations of reasoning may vary. Possibilities include:
      a. 0.28 is about **1/4** because 0.28 is about 0.25 and 0.25 = 25/100 = 1/4.
      b. 3.125 is about **3 1/10** because 0.125 rounds to .1.
      c. 0.03939.. is about **4/100 = 2/50 = 1/25** because 0.039 rounds to 0.04.
      d. .99... **is 1.** Let n = 0.999.... Then 10n = 9.999.... and 10n -n = 9 n = 9.999... - 0.999... = 9. Thus n = 1.

15. Responses will vary. A possibility is: 0.3 is the decimal representation of 3/10 and 0.30 is the decimal representation of 30/100. But applying the Fundamental Theorem of Fractions to 3/10 by multiplying both numerator and denominator by 10, we get 3/10 = 30/100. Since the fractions represent the same number the equivalent decimal representation also represent the same number.

17. Responses will vary. One possibility is to represent the project with the number 1. Then if n students show up and commit to the project for the month, each student should do about 1/n of the work. If the project is anticipated to take h hours, the each student should plan on working (1/n) (h) hours.

19. Responses will vary. Possible responses include: In both the rational and the whole numbers, the other numbers are based on 1. In the whole number system, the other numbers are multiples of 1, in the rational number system the other numbers are parts of 1. 1 is the multiplicative identity in both systems. In the system of rationals there are infinitely many representation of 1 (2/2, 3/3, etc.).

21. Responses will vary. The facts are that 1/13 of the women on one campus were polled and 48/1000 responded that they would prefer to attend all female mathematics classes. On the other campus 1/5 of the women students were polled and 48/1000 of those polled said yes.

23. Responses will vary. One possibility is: Adding 0's to the right of a decimal digit is adding 0 times a unitary part of some power of 10. But 0 time any number is 0. Thus when appending 0's one is actually adding 0's and 0 is the additive identity.

25.

Fraction	Decimal representation
1/7	0 .142857142.
2/7	0.285714285
3/7	0.428571428
4/7	0.571428571.
5/7	0.714285714
6/7	0.857142857
7/7	1.

a. b. c. d. Responses may vary. The decimal representations of 2/7, 3/7, 4/7, 5/7, 7/7, and 7/7 are not the corresponding multiples of the decimal display for 1/7 if that display is reentered. However, if the display is the result of dividing 1 by 7 and that result is directly used in the multiplications by 1, 2, etc. the corresponding display are matched. Even though rounding will occur, the calculator maintains numbers to a greater accuracy than it displays. Moreover the quotient of 1 divided by 7 is an infinitely repeating decimal. When a number is entered from the keyboard it is necessarily finite.

27. Responses will vary. A possibility is: The Stevin notation is akin to our expanded notation. Stevin's representation of 325/1000 is (3 x one tenth unit) + (2 x one hundredth unit) + (5 x one thousandth unit). It is as if the circled numbers are negative exponents for powers of 10

29. a. The women's wage, w, is 3/4 of the men's wage, m: w = (3/4) m Now, w + (1/4) w = (5/4)w. This is a 25% increase in pay. But (5/4)w = (5/4)(3/4)m = 15/16 m. This is still less than the men's wage.
    b. Suppose that both the men's and women's wages are daily and based on an 8 hour day. Let w and m represent these daily wages. If m and w stay constant but the women's work day is reduced to 6 hours, the hourly wage for women becomes w/6 and the men's hourly wage is m/8. But w is (3/4)m. So the women's hourly wage can be represented (3/4)m÷6 = m/8. So the second strategy equalizes the hourly wages. But the gross earnings of women will still be 3/4 of those of men.

c.

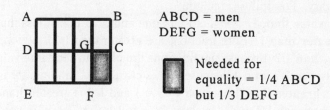

ABCD = men
DEFG = women

Needed for
equality = 1/4 ABCD
but 1/3 DEFG

SECTION 6.2

1.

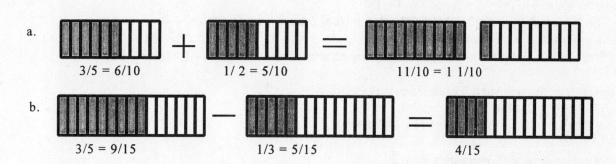

a.   3/5 = 6/10   +   1/ 2 = 5/10   =   11/10 = 1 1/10

b.   3/5 = 9/15   −   1/3 = 5/15   =   4/15

c. Same as (a) because 0.6 = 3/5 and 0.5 = 1/2.

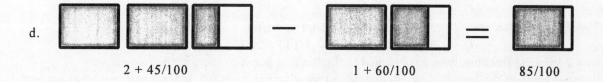

d.   2 + 45/100   −   1 + 60/100   =   85/100

3. a. **20/3**   b. **-19/4**   c. **17/2**   d. **109/10**

5. a. 7 5/6 + 2 2/5 = (7 + 2) + 5/6 + 2/5 = 9 + 25/30 + 12/30 = 9 + 37/30 = **10 7/30**.
    b. 3/4 + 4/5 + 5/6 = 45/60 + 48/60 + 50/60 = **143/60 = 2 23/60**.
    c. 9 1/8 - 6 5/6 = (9 - 6) + (1/8 - 5/6) = 3 + (3/24 - 20/24) = 3 + (-17/24) = 2 + 24/24 - 17/24 = **2 7/24**.
    d. 7/8 - 5/6 = 21/24 - 20/24 = **1/24**.
    e. 5.9 - 2.14 + 1.008 = 5.900 - 2.140 + 1.008 = **4.768**.
    f. 7.8 - 4.386 = 7.800 - 4.386 = **3.414.**

7. a. 24.6 + 3.09 = 24 + 6/10 + 3 + 9/100 = 240/10 + 6/10 + 300/100 + 9/100 =
        2400/100 + 60/100 + 300/100 + 9/100 = (2400 + 60 + 300 + 9)/100 = 2769/100 = **27.69**.
    b.   24.60
         +   3.09
              27.69
    c   Because the same 2 numbers were added in both cases and because the sum is a unique number, **the sums
        are the same**. Discussions will vary but students may note that the decimal algorithm seems quicker and
        less prone to error.

9.   Explanations will vary. Possibilities include:
   a.   7/9 + 6/13 is **greater than 1**. 7/9 is close to one and 6/13 is just less than a half.
   b.   4/6 + 6/7 is **greater than 1**. Both fractions are greater than 1/2.
   c.   4/5 - 3/4 is **less than 1/2** because the fractions are close to the same value.
   d.   3/7 + 2/9 is **between 1/2 and 1** because 3/7 is close to 1/2 adding 2/9 is less than 1/2.
   e.   4 1/5 - 3 1/20 is **greater than 1** because 4 - 3 = 1 and 1/5 is greater than 1/20.
   f.   7 3/7 - 6 2/3 is **between 1/2 and 1** because 7 - 6 is 1 but 3/7 and 2/3 are near ½ but 2/3 is greater than 3/7.

11.   First we must find the sizes of all the pieces relative to the large triangles (a or b) represented by 1.   Since
      parts a and b fit exactly on each other and a = 1, **b** =1 also. Now, c and e are identical, c and e fill d, c and e
      also fill g, and c, d, and e fill b. So **c = 1/4, e = 1/4, d = 1/2, and g = 1/2**.   Since c, d, ,e, f, and g   fill a + b,
      the sum 1/4 + ½ + 1/4 + f + ½ = 2. So **f = 1/2.**
   a.   So **b + c + d + e + f = 1 + 1/4 + 1/2 + 1/4 + 1/2 = 2 1/2.**
   b.   **a + d + e = 1 + 1/2+ 1/4 = 1 3/4.**
   c.   Since only a and g are missing, the figure has an area of 4, **4 - a - g = 4 - 1 - 1/2 = 2 1/2.**

13.   Counterexample will vary. Possibilities include:
   a.   3/4 - 1/4 = 2/4 but 1/4 - 3/4 = - 2/4.
   b.   (7/8 - 4/8) - 1/8 = 2/8 but 7/8 - (4/8 - 1/8) = 4/8.

15. Responses will vary. Possibilities include:
   a.   17.51 and 57.52;   9.23 and 65.8;   87.98 and -12.95 all add to 75.03.
   b.   The first number was randomly chosen. The other of the pair was obtained by subtracting the first from
        75.03.

17. a.   The next two rows are: 1/6   1/30   1/60   1/60   1/30   1/6
                                    1/7 1/42   1/105   1/140   1/105   1/42   1/7
   b.   Any 2 adjacent fractions have a sum equal to the fraction between them in the row above.
   c.   Because some of the fractions are equivalent to repeating decimals the patterns may not be as evident.

                                  1
                          0.5   0.5
                    0.3...   0.16..   0.3...
                0.25   0.083...   0.083... 0.25
            0.2   0.05   0.03...   0.05   0.2

19. Calculators perform computations in fraction form. 7/12 is the simplest form of the sum of 1/3 and 1/4.
   b   Another press of '=' will display **19/12**.
   c.   Responses will vary. One solution is to count: 19/12 (5 times), 22/12 (6 times), ...34/12 (**10 times**).
   d.   **No**. There is no integer n such that 7 + 3n = 69.

21. a.   1/5 - 2/9 = 9/45 - 10/45 = -1/45. **-1/45 is the result of the computation.**
   b.   Each time the '=' key is pressed another 2/9 = 10/45 is subtracted from the dispaly. The next 2 presses
        will display **-31/45, then -41/45.**
   c.   Each time the '=' key is pressed the numerator decreases by 10. So counting down to -81 we have: -21 (3
        presses), -31 (4 presses), -41 (5 presses), ... -81 (9 presses). N/D --> n/d will appear when the numerator
        and denominator have a common factor other than 1. This symbol indicates that the fraction in the display
        is not in simplest form.

23. Responses will vary. Possibilities include:
   a.   Because 1/3 + 1/4 + 1/6 is about 3/4, the $600 is about 1/4 of the total. So the total was about 4 times $600 or $2400.
   b.

      Loans (1/3)
      Entertainment (1/6)
      Clothes (1/4)
      Savings ($600)

   c.   Let I represent the inheritance. Then **[1 - (1/4 + 1/6 + 1/3)]I = 600.** (12/12 - 3/12 - 2/12 - 4/12)I = 600. So (3/12) I = (1/4)I = 600 and **I = 2400.**

25. Responses will vary. A possibility is: By lining up the decimal points the numbers in a column are all multiples of the same power of ten. Thus by adding up the numbers in the columns the distributive law is being applied.

27. Responses will vary. A possibility is:

2 1/4 + 3 1/3 = 2 + 1/4 + 3 + 1/3	symbolism convention for mixed numbers
= 2 + (1/4 + 3) + 1/3	associative property of addition
= 2 + (3 + 1/4) + 1/3	commutative property of addition
= (2 + 3) + (1/4 + 1/3)	associative property of addition
= 5 + 7/12	simplification
= 5 7/12	numeral convention

29. · a.   **4/1 + 3/2 = 5 1/2.**
   b.   **8/5 + 7/6 = 83/30 = 2 23/30**
   c.   **9/2 + 8/5 = 61/10 = 6 1/10.**
   d.   If the integers a, b, c, d are all positive and are ordered smallest to largest, a < b < c < d then the **largest sum** will be obtained by adding **(d/a) + (c/b).**

31. a.   For the integers 1, 2, 3, and 4 guess-check-revise give **(4/1) - (2/3) = 3 1/3** as the greatest difference.
   b.   The same method applied to 5, 6, 7, and 8 gives **(8/5) - (6/7) = 26/35.**
   c.   Guess-check-revise applied to 2, 5, 8, and 9 gives **(9/2) - (5/8) = 31/8.**
   d.   With the integers such that 0 < a < b < c < d, the greatest difference appears to be given by **(d/a) - (b/c).**

33. a.   If an integer were 0, because division by 0 is not a defined operation, the 0 could not in the denominator of a fraction.
   b.   If an integer were negative then the value of the fraction containing that integer would be negative. If the integers are still ordered a < b < c < d for the largest sum we have : with a -, d/b + a/c; with b or c -, d/a + b/c; and with d -, c/b + a/d. For the smallest sum we have: with a or d -, d/a + b/c; with b -, b/a + c/d; and with c -, c/a + b/d. For the largest difference: a or d, -, c/b - d/a and for b or c -, b/a - c/b. For the smallest difference and with a or d -, d/a - c/b and with c or b -, c/b - d/a.

35. Responses will vary among students. The common denominator obtained by multiplying the given denominators is easy to find and makes algorithmic computation easy. However, the result of the computation is frequently not in simplest terms.

37. Responses will vary. Possibilities include:
   a.   If the denominators, b and d, are equal, then either is the least common denominator.
   b.   If either is a factor of the other, then the larger of the 2 denominators is the least common denominator.
   c.   If b and have common factors that appear only once is each denominator then the least common denominator is the product of b and d divided by each of the common factors. If the common factors appear more than once in each denominator then the least common denominator is the product of the denominators divided by the common factor the fewer of the number of times it appears in the individual denominators.
   d.   If the denominators have no common factors other than 1, the least common denominator is the product of the 2 denominators.

SECTION 6.3

1.
   a.
      2/3 ($\boxed{/\!/}$) $\boxed{}$ = 6/15 ($\boxed{\times\times}$)
      x   3/5 ($\boxed{\backslash\backslash}$)

   b.   3/2 x 3/4 =   (1 + 1/2) 3/4 =   3/4 + 1/2 (3/4)

      $\boxed{}$ + $\boxed{}$ = 9/8 ($\boxed{\times\times}$)

      3/4($\boxed{\backslash\backslash}$) x 1($\boxed{/\!/}$)   1/2($\boxed{\backslash\backslash}$) x 3/4($\boxed{/\!/}$)

   c.
      2/3 ($\boxed{/\!/}$) $\boxed{}$ = 6/6 = 1 ($\boxed{\times\times}$)
      x   3/2 ($\boxed{\backslash\backslash}$)

   d.
      3/4 ($\boxed{/\!/}$) $\boxed{}$ = 9/16 ($\boxed{\times\times}$)
      x   3/4 ($\boxed{\backslash\backslash}$)

3.   a.   2 1/3 x 3/7 = 7/3 x 3/7 = **1**.
   b.   (2 3/4 + 1 1/2)(2/3) = (3 + 3/4 + 1/2)(2/3) = (3 + 1 1/4)(2/3) = (4 + 1/4)(2/3) = (17/4)(2/3) = **17/6 = 2 5/6**.
   c.   16.025 x 0.4 = **6.41**.
   d.   -3/5 x 3 ½ = -3/5 x 7/2 = **-21/10 = -2 1/10**.
   e.   (ab/c)(c²a/b) =a²bc²/bc = **a²c**.
   f.   3/4 x 4.8 = 0.75 x 4.8 = **3.6** = 3/4 x 4 8/10 = 3/4 x 48/10 = **144/40 = 72/20 = 36/10 = 18/5 = 3 3/5**.

5.   Responses will vary. Examples are:
   a.   If 1/3 of a class is over 21 and 1/4 of those students age-eligible are registered to vote, what fraction of the class can vote in the next election.
   b.   Find the area of a surface 2.5 by 3.5 meters.
   c.   If 1/3 of your stock portfolio has decreased by 150%, the other holdings remaining constant, what is the change in the value of your holdings?
   d.   Seven brothers had 7 dollars to give equally to 7 brides. How much money did each bride receive?

7.   The multiplicative inverse of a number x is the number y such that (x)(y) = 1.
   a.   (5/8)(**8/5**) = 1
   b.   -3 3/11 = -36/11: (-36/11)(**-11/36**) = 1
   c.   0.15 = 15/100: (15/100)(**100/15**) = 1   **100/15 = 6 2/3**
   d.   9.18 = 918/100: (918/100)(**100/918**) = 1
   e.   (1/2 + 1/3)(1/2 + 2/3) = (5/6)(7/6) = 35/36: (35/36)(**36/35**) = 1.
   f.   (-x)(**1/-x**) = 1 unless x = 0 in which case there is no multiplicative inverse.

9.   Estimates and reasoning will vary. Some possibilities include:
    a.   (3/4) ? = 16. The missing factor is around 20 because 3/4 is between ½ and 1 so the missing factor is between 16 and 32.
    b.   ? (.25) = 0.5. The missing factor is 2 by inspection and knowledge of number facts.
    c.   (-4/3) ? = 2/3. The missing factor is -1/2 by inspection and knowledge of number facts. It must be negative to produce a positive product.
    d.   (5/6) ? = 1.5. The missing factor is around 2 because 5/6 is between ½ and 1.

11.   This is **false**. 0 is a rational number and yet has no multiplicative inverse because 1/0 is not defined.

13.   The purpose of the process is to produce a rational number that is easily simplified before multiplying. thus making the multiplication easier. **It is always valid** as shown by the following representative argument. Let a/b and c/d be two rational numbers to be multiplied. The (a/b)(c/d) = (ac)/(bd) by the definition of rational number multiplication. The product (ac)/(bd) = (ac)/(db) [because multiplication is commutative] = (a/d)(c/b) by the converse of the definition of rational number multiplication.

15.   Responses will vary. Examples are:
    a.   (6)(10)(1/6) = 10;   (5)(11)(10/55) = 10;   To find the factors pick any 2 non-zero numbers, say a and b, as the first 2 factors . To find the third factor, f, solve the equation abf = 10.
    b.   The 3 factors could be length, width, and height of a right-angled box with a volume of 10

17.   a.   N/D --> n/d indicates that the fraction in the display is not in its simplest form.
    b.   Since each time the '='key is pressed the display is multiplied by ½ the next two keypresses would display: N/D --> n/d   2/48 and N/D --> n/d   2/96.
    c.   Each press of the '=' key doubles the denominator beginning with 6. So **8** successive keypresses produce 2/6, 2/12, 2/24, 2/48, 2/96, 2/192, 2/384, 2/768.
    d.   The display N/D --> n/d   2/246 **will not appear** in this sequence because 2/246 is not equivalent to the product (2/3) x (1/2)^x for any integer value of x.

19.   a.   The value, V, decreases by **1/(27 1/2) = 1/(55/2) = 2/55** each year.
    b.   The depreciation the first year is (2/55)(85,000) =**$3090.91** to the nearest cent.

21.   Responses will vary. Possibilities include:
    a.   The conjecture that 'multiplication makes numbers bigger' most probably arises from experience with natural numbers. For example the product of 3 and 4 is larger than either 3 or 4.
    b.   The conjecture is true if multiplication is restricted to the set of natural numbers.
    c.   It is false when multiplying whole numbers (0 x 6 = 0), integers (-2 x 3 = -6) and rational numbers (1/2 x 1/3 = 1/6).

23.   Responses will vary. A possibility is:
        (2 3/5) x (1 1/4) = (2 + 3/5)(1 + 1/4)   convention for the representation of mixed numbers.
        = 2(1) + 2(1/4) + 3/5(1) + (3/5)(1/4)   distributive property
        = 2 + ½ + 3/5 + 3/20   rational number multiplication
        = 2 + 10/20 + 12/20+ 3/20   Fundamental Theorem of Fractions
        = 2 + 25/20 = **3 1/4**   arithmetic simplification

25.   a.   The least product is (1/3)(2/4) = (1/4)(2/3) = **2/12 = 1/6**.
    b.   The least product is (6/7)(5/8) = (5/7)(6/8) = **30/56 = 15/28**.
    c.   The least product is (2/8)(5/9) = (5/8)(2/9) = **10/72 = 5/36**.
    d.   If 0 < a < b < c < d, the least product is given by **(ab)/(cd)**.

27. a. $(1/2)(1/4) = (1 \times 1)/(2 \times 4) = \mathbf{1/8}$. In decimal for the product is $(0.5)(0.25) = \mathbf{0.125}$. The products are equally accurate because 0.125, a terminating decimal, is an exact representation of the rational 1/8.

  b. $(1/3)(2/3)$ is **2/9**. The multiplication algorithm cannot be applied to the decimal representations of 1/3 and 2/3.

29. a.   The probability of two consecutive sixes is $(1/6)(1/6) = \mathbf{1/36}$.

  b.   The probability is $(1/50)(1/49) = \mathbf{1/2450}$.

  c.   The probability is $(0.1)(0.1)(0.1)(0.1) = \mathbf{.0001 = 1/10,000}$.

SECTION 6.4

1. a.
```
 0        1        2        3
|__|__|__|__|__|__|__|__|__|__|__|
<====><====><====><==>
 1(2/3)  1(2/3)  1(2/3 ) ½(2/3)
```
   $2\ 1/3 \div 2/3 = 3\ 1/2$

  b.
```
 0                1/2  3/5              1
|__|__|__|__|__|__|_|__|__|__|__|__|
<==============><==>
 1(1/ 2)            1/5(1/ 2)
```
   $3/5 \div 1/2 = 1\ 1/5$

  c.
```
 0          3          6          9          12
|_____|_____|_____|_____|
==>==>==>==>==>==>==>==>==>==>==>==>==>==>==>==>
 16 (3/4)'s completely fill the length 12.
```
   $12 \div 3/4 = 16$

  d.
```
 0                1                2
|__|__|__|__|__|__|__|__|__|__|__|__|
<==============><=>|===|===|==|===|
 1 (5/6)          1/5 (5/6)
```
   $1 \div 5/6 = 1\ 1/5$

3.   Explanations will vary. Possibilities include: Only **b and c** are determined by $4 \div 3/4$. (b) can be viewed as 4 yds = (number of pieces) x (each 3/4 yd long). So the number of pieces is $4 \div 3/4$. In (c) we have 4 rotations in 3/4 of an hour which can be represented as (4 rot)/[(3/4) x 1 hr] = [4/(3/4)rot/1 hr]. (a) would be determined by calculating $(3/4) \div 4$ and (d) by $(3/4) \times 4$.

5.   a.   The quotient by the common denominator method is: $3/4 \div 2/5 = (3 \times 5)/(4 \times 5) \div (2 \times 4)/(5 \times 4) = (3 \times 5)/(2 \times 4) = \mathbf{15/8}$.

  b.   The quotient by the complex fraction method is: $3/4 \div 2/5 = (3/4)/(2/5) = (3/4 \times 5/2)/ (2/5 \times 5/2) = (15/8)/1 = \mathbf{15/8}$.

  c.   The quotient by the missing factor method is: $3/4 = 2/5 \times f$. So f x 5/2 x 2/5 = 3/4 x 5/2 ; f = **15/8**.

  d.   The quotient by "Invert and multiply" is: $3/4 \div 2/5 = 3/4 \times 5/2 = \mathbf{15/8}$.

7.   The methods chosen will vary.

  a. $9/10 \div 2/3 = 9/10 \times 3/2 = \mathbf{27/20}$.

  b. $4\ ½ \div 5\ 1/4 = 9/2 \div 21/4 = 9/2 \times 4/21 = \mathbf{6/7}$.

  c. $-14.68 \div 1.9 = \mathbf{-7.726315789}$ by calculator.

  d. $1 \div 4/5 = 1 \times 5/4 = \mathbf{5/4 = 1\ 1/4}$.

9.   Responses will vary. Possibilities include:
   a.   5/6 = 40/48 = 80/96 and 7/8 = 42/48 = 84/96. So 5/6 < **81/96 < 82/96 < 83/96** < 7/8.
   b.   13/15 = 52/60 and 14/15 = 56/60. So 13/15 < **53/60 < 54/60 < 55/60** < 14/15.
   c.   -0.2 < **-0.199 < -0.198 < -0.197** < -0.1
   d.   -1/4 < **-1/8 < 0 < 1/8** < 1/4.

11. Reasoning will vary among students. Quotients **greater than 1 are b, c, and d: 3/4 ÷ 2/3** because 3/4 is
    closer to 1 that is 2/3, **14 ÷ 2/3** because 2/3 is close to 1, and **5.6 ÷ 4.9** because the dividend is larger than the
    divisor.
    The quotient **between ½ and 1 is (a), 3 2/9 ÷ 5 1/7,** because the dividend is more than half of the divisor. The
    quotient **1 ÷ 8/3, (e), is less than ½** because 8/3 is greater than 2. The quotient **(f), .1 ÷ .2, equals** 1/2.

13. Reasoning will vary. Possibilities include:
   a.   691.04 ÷ 5.6 = **123.400** because 500 ÷ 5 = 100.
   b.   69.104 ÷ 56 = **1.23400** because 60 is bigger than 50.
   c.   0.69104 ÷ 0.56 = **1.23400** because .6 is greater than .5 but not double.
   d.   691.04 ÷ 56 = **12.3400** because 600 ÷ 50 is greater than 10.

15. a.   Every time the '=' key is pressed the display is divided 3/4. So the next press of '=' will display the result
        of 64/27 ÷ 3/4 = **256/81**.
    b   The sequence of displays is 4/3, 16/9, 64/27, 256,81, 1024/243, 4096/729. So 4096/729 appears on the
        sixth press of '='.
    c.   If the key sequence been 1, +, 3, /, 4 the display would have been 1 3/4 because of order of operations.

17. Responses will vary. Some possibilities are:
    a. 0.1, **0.1313...** 0.2   b. -4.74, **-4.732121...** -4.73   c. 3/5, **0.7979...,** 4/5   d. -1/4, **0.123123...,** 1/4.

19. Responses will vary. A possibility is: Suppose a/b is a rational number with a reciprocal between 0 and 1.
    Then 0 < b/a < 1. b/a is less than 1, the reciprocal of b/a, 1/(b/a) = a/b, is greater than 1. Thus any number
    greater than 1 has a reciprocal between 0 and 1. So the set of numbers with reciprocals between 0 and 1 is all
    the rational numbers that are greater than 1.

21. Responses will vary. Possibilities include:
    a,   If we are restricted to the set of natural numbers, then division of a number generally results in a smaller
        number. The exception is division by 1. Thus the conjecture that division, generally, makes numbers
        smaller.
    b.   The conjecture is true within the integers in all cases in which the dividend is positive and the divisor is
        greater than 1 (example: 6 ÷ 3 = 2) or when the dividend is positive and the divisor negative
        (example: 6 ÷ -2 = -12; -12 < 6).
    c.   It is false within the integers if both dividend and divisor are less than 0, for example -6 ÷ -2 = 3 and
        3 > -6. It is also false when the dividend is less than zero and the divisor is greater than 1, for example
        -6 ÷ 2 = -3: -3 > -6.

23. a.   i. 1÷3/4 = **4/3**   ii. 1÷5/6 = **6/5**   iii. 1÷3/7 = **7/3**   iv. 1÷4/9 = **9/4**.
    b.   The pattern suggests that **1÷a/b = b/a.**
    c.   1÷a/b = 1/(a/b) = [1/(a/b)] x [(b/a)/(b/a)] = [1(b/a)]/[(a/b)(b/a)] = (b/a)/[(ba/ab)] (b/a)/1 = b/a for all non-
        zero integers a and b.

25. a.   The number of square feet may be determined by dividing the asking price by the price per square foot.
    b.   The square footages are, respectively, **1532, 1198, 1689, 1280, 1598, 3190.**
    c.   **E3 = B3 ÷ D3 , E4 = B4 ÷ D4, ..., E8 = B8 ÷ D8**
    c.   i. The costs in dollars per square foot are now, respectively, **52.81, 53.84, 42.92, 57.03, 53.75, 56.39.**
         ii. **F3 = (B3 - 2000) ÷ F3, F4 = (B4 - 2000) ÷ F4, ..., F8 = (B8 - 2000) ÷ F8**
    d.   **B9 =(B3 + B4 + B5 + B6 +B7 + B8)/6** . When one of a data set is much higher or lower than the rest of the data an arithmetic average is not appropriate because that one value has a disproportionate effect on the average. These conditions apply with this data.

27. a.   The greatest quotient is obtained by **(4/1) ÷ (2/3) = 6.**
    b.   The greatest quotient is obtained by **(8/5) ÷ (6/7) = 28/15.**
    c.   The greatest quotient is obtained from **(9/2) ÷ (5/8) = 7 1/5.**
    d.   if $0 < a < b < c < d$ then the greatest quotient is obtained from the expression **(d/a) ÷ (b/c)** or the equivalent **(c/b) ÷ (a/d)**. Both quotients are (dc)/(ab).

29. a.   If one of the integers is 0 the only acceptable quotient is 0.
    b.   The least and greatest quotients reverse because the they will be negative.
    c.   The results depend on the order of the absolute values and if there is an even or odd numbers of negatives.

31. The sugar in recipe 1 is 2/3 cup per 6 servings or 1/9 cup per serving. The sugar is recipe 2 is 3/4 cup per 8 servings or 3/32 cup per serving, a bit less than 1/10 cup per serving. So recipe 1 has more sugar per serving.

33. a.   3(1/3) = (3/1)(1/3) = (3)(1)/(1)(3) = 1= 3(0.3333...) = 0.999...
    b.   9(1/9) = 1 = 9(.111...) = 0.9999.....
    c.   0.99... = 9(1/9) [from problem 32 a] = 1

35. Responses will vary. A possible argument is: Assume that a/b < c/d. Then 1/2(a/b) < 1/2(c/d). So 1/2(a/b) + 1/2(c/d) < 1/2(c/d) + 1/2(c/d) = c/d. Similarly, 1/2(c/d) > 1/2(a/b) and 1/2(c/d) + 1/2(a/b) > 1/2(a/b) + 1/2(a/b) = a/b. Thus the arithmetic mean, (a/b + c/d)/2 = 1/2(a/b) + 1/2(c/d) is greater than a/b and less than c/d and therefore lies between a/b and c/d. As an example, let a/b = 4/10 and c/d = 8/10. 1/2(4/10) = 2/10, 1/2(8/10) = 4/10, and 1/2(4/10 + 8/10) = 6/10. 2/10 < 6/10 < 8/10.

37. a.   The expression is: R = (h+3)/(b+3).
    b.   Let r = h/b = 1/3. Then R = 4/6 and R > r. Let r be 4/6. Then R = 7/9 and again R > r. It appears that if a positive integer is added to the numerator and denominator of a fraction the value of the fraction increases.

39. a.   2/3 ÷ 5/6 = 4/5. Because the decimal representations of both rational numbers are repeating, there is no algorithm for the computation.
    b.   ½ ÷ 3/5 = 5/6. .5 ÷ 0.6 = 0.83333... (by calculator). Both representations are equivalent because 5/6 is the repeating decimal 0.833...

41. a.   Estimates will vary. 1.4 is a possibility. 1.4 x 1.4 = 1.96.
    b.   Since 1.96 < 2, raise the estimate to, say, 1.41. 1.41 x 1.41 = 1.9881
    c.   Again revising upwards: 1.412 x 1.412 = 1.993744. Try 1.414 x 1.414 = 1.999396. Try 1.4145 x 1.4145 = 2.00081025.

d. Suppose that you could express $\sqrt{2} = a/b$. Then $2 = (a/b)^2 = a^2/b^2$. So $2 b^2 = a^2$. Now suppose that the prime factorization of a contained some number of 2's. Then a x a would contain double that number of 2's. So the number of 2's in the prime factorization of a^2 is either 0 or even. Applying the same argument to b^2 we see that the number of 2's in the prime factorization of $2 b^2$ is 1 or some other odd number. But a^2 is equal to $2b^2$ and the prime factorization of a number is unique. Thus $(a/b)^2$ cannot be equal to 2 and the square root of 2 cannot be represented with a rational number.

CHAPTER 6 REVIEW EXERCISES

1.

a.

5/8

b.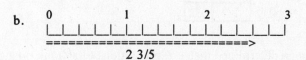

2 3/5

c.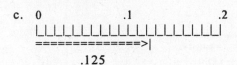

.125

3.
Fraction form	Decimal form	Method of Solution
5/12	**0.4166...**	by calculator
125/999	0.125...	n = 0.125..., 1000 n = 125.125..., 999n = 125, n = 125/999
56/100	0.56	definition of decimal notation

5.
	Number	Additive Inverse	Multiplicative Inverse
a.	2/3	**-2/3**	**3/2**
b.	-4/3	**4/3**	**-3/4**
c.	0.25	**-0.25**	**1/.25**
d.	0	**0**	**not defined**

7. a.. 2 1/10 x -8 1/3 = 21/10 x -25/3 = **- 35/2 = 17 1/2**.
   b. 7 1/8 x 6 1/4 = 57/8 x 25/4 =**1425/32 = 44 17/32**.
   c. .04 x 6.001 = **0.24004** by calculator
   d. 2.04 x 3.25 = **6.63** by calculator

9. Responses will vary. Some example word problems are:
   a. One brand of instant potatoes calls for 1 3/4 cup of water and 1 ½ cup milk. How much liquid does the recipe require? s = 1 3/4 + 1 ½ = **3 1/4.**

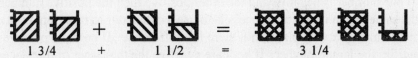

1 3/4   +   1 1/2   =   3 1/4

b.   In the above recipe how much more water than milk is required? **d = 1 3/4 - 1 ½ = 1/4.**

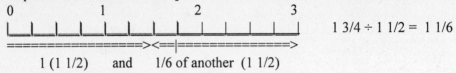

1 3/4   -   1 1/ 2   =   1/4

c.   A rectangular piece of wood is 1 3/4 yd by 1 1/2 yd. What is the area?   **p = 1 3/4 x 1 ½ = 2 5/8 sq yd.**

$$1 \frac{1}{2} \times 1 \frac{3}{4} = 1 + \frac{3}{4} + \frac{1}{2} + \frac{3}{8} = 2 \frac{5}{8}$$

d.   It has been determined that 1 ½ revolutions of a crank on a car jack can lift a car 1 3/4 in. How many revolutions are required to lift the car 1 in? **q = 1 3/4 ÷ 1 ½ = 7/4 x 2/3 = 14/12 = 1 1/6**

1 3/4 ÷ 1 1/2 = 1 1/6

1 (1 1/2)   and   1/6 of another (1 1/2)

11.   2.357... **is a rational number**. Every rational number can also be represented as either a terminating decimal or, as in this case, a repeating decimal.

13.   a.   Methods of estimation will vary. One is: the sum of the weights S = (1/2 + 6 3/4) + 2 3/4 + 2 1/8 + 1 is approximately 7 + 2 + 3 + 1 = 13. So the groceries should be put into 2 sacks.
       b.   Responses will vary. One possibility is: Since the total is about 13 lbs and the ham weighs about half of the total, put the ham in one bag and the remainder of the groceries in another bag.

15.   a.   Explanations will vary. One possibility is: Martha's statement is **false**. If her old salary is represented by S and her new salary by N then N = (3/4) S. Expressing her new salary as a difference: S - (1/4) S = (3/4)S. So her salary was **reduced by 1/4.**
       b.   Since her new salary, N, is (3/4) S we have N = (3/4) S or S = (4/3)N = N + (1/3) N. So her new salary would have to be increased by a third to again be equal to her original salary.

17.   Responses will vary. A possibility is; **Both are correct**. When a division by 5 produces the result 32 R 2 it means 32 groups of 5 and 2 ungrouped units. A display of 32.4 when the quotient of a division by 5 means 32 groups of 5 and 4/10 of a group of 5. But 4/10 of a group of 5 is (4/10)5 = 2. So the displays are different representations of the same quotient.

19.   Responses will vary. If one number is negative and the other positive then the positive number is the larger. If the numbers are of the same sign an efficient process is to use a calculator to represent both rationals as decimals. Compare the decimals place by place until there is a difference. If both are positive then the larger of the place values identifies the larger number. If both are negative the the larger of the place values identifies the smaller number. If the calculator does not show a difference represent both as rationals with a common denominator and compare the numerators as the place values were described.

21.   Responses will vary depending on student-student interactions.

SECTION 7.1

1. The ratio girls : boys = **3 : 4**. The ratio students : boys = **7 : 4**; the ratio students : girls = **7 : 3.**

3. 8 successes : 10 attempts = x successes : 15 attempts = y successes : 20 attempts = z successes : 75 attempts.
    So 8/10 = x/15; x = (8/10)15 = 120/10 = **12 successes**. Similarly, y = **16 successes**, z = **60 successes**.

5.

c	d	
6	2	c/d = 3/1 = 6/d. So 3 d = 6 and d = 6/3 = 2.
9.3	3	c/d = 3/1 = c/3. So c = 3 x 3 = 9.
10	**3 1/3**	c/d = 3/1 = 10/d. So 3 d = 10 and d = 10/3.
27	9	c/d = 3/1 = c/9. So c = 9 x 3 = 27.
21	7	c/d = 3/1 = 21/d. So 3d = 21 and d 21/3 = 7.
12	4	c/d = 3/1 = c/4. So c = 12.

7. Responses will vary. One possibility is: 2/1 < 2x/5 < 3/1 is equivalent to 10/5 < 2x/5 < 15/5. So 2x must be between 10 and 15. Since x must be an integer, **x = 6 or 7.**

9. Let A represent 2.5 run per 9 innings. Let B represent the ratio 2 runs per 6 innings. Then B = (2/6)run/inn = x runs / 9 innings.   So 2 / 6 = x / 9 and 6x = 18. So x = 3. Thus his last performance is equivalent to 3 runs per nine innings, **worse** that his performance up to the last game.

11. Assuming that the drop of the line is proportional to its length and letting D represent the drop, we have the proportion 1/40 = D/100. 40 D =100; **D = 2 ½ ft.**

13. Responses will vary. Possibilities include: 72 beats per 60 seconds = **12 beats / 10 sec = 6/5 sec.**

15. a. If the cost is $1.80 for 1.2 liters the unit price is $1.80/1.2 l = **$1.50 per liter.**
    b. The unit price is $1.20/ 3 = **$0.40 each**.
    c. The unit price is 86 cents/2 = **43 cents each**.
    d. The unit price is $1.60/0.5 kg = **$3.20 per kg**.

17. The ratio of foreign car drivers to interviewees is 0 to 20.

19. Let h represent the number of hits needed in the next 10 at bats to get an average of 0.300. Then
    (148 + h)/(500 + 10) = 0.3. So 148 + h = 510(0.3) = 153. Thus h = 153 - 148 = **5**.

21. Arguments will vary. Since the number of units is determined by dividing cost by unit price, and since the unit prices are the same, the greater cost is associated with the greater number of items.   The ratio of the numbers of units is = the ratio of the costs. So number A to number B = **10 : 8 = 5:4**.

23. Responses will vary. Possibilities include the argument: If one is comparing unit prices, that is cost per unit, then the lower ratio is the better buy because one is spending less money for a fixed amount of product. But if one compares amount of product for unit of money, then the product with the larger ratio is the better buy.
    a. **Juanita is correct** because Bill's computation is not the price per unit product but rather the number of units of product for a fixed price.
    b. The problem could have been solved by comparing unit prices.
    c. Responses will vary. The students might consider the dimensions of the computation. They have divided amount by price so the dimensions are ounces per dollar. The consumer wants the greatest amount of product per dollar spent. So the 128 oz is the better buy, 40.125 oz/dollar.

25.   The ratio 1/3 : 1 is equal to (1/3)(3/1)/1(3/1) = **1 : 3**.

27.   A cost of $2.00 per 7.8 oz is about $2.00 per 8 oz or **about 25 cents per oz for the large size**. A cost of $1.50 for 6.1 oz is about $1.50 for 6 oz or also **about 25 cents per oz for the small size**.   However, the estimate for the large size was an overestimate (because 7.8 < 8) and that for the small size is an underestimate (because 6.1 > 6). So the **small size is the better buy**. The actual unit prices are: **large: 25.6 cents/oz, small 24.6 cents/oz**.

29.   **Jackie's results are acceptable**. The ratio of RCA to Sony to Panasonic 3 : 5 : 4. It is possible that one person owns more than 1 television and that these are different brands. There could easily be 12 sets owned among 10 persons. It might clarify matters if Jackie referred to the ratio of RCA sets *owned* to Sony sets *owned* rather than to the ratio of RCA set owners and Sony set owners.

31.   Responses will vary. The facts are that the ratio of firearms per owner is 4.5 : 1. If there are 50 million firearm owners then there are about 225 million privately owned firearms in the country.

33.   Specific responses will vary. The facts are: The sales values, in thousands of dollars, are about 15 per 1 year, 30 per 2 years, 45 per 3 years and 60 per 4 years. The ratio of sales to time in years is constant. This graph shows no growth (or decline) in sales.

SECTION 7.2

1.   If 2 quantities, say y and x, vary proportionally then y = kx, k a constant, for all values of y and x. So, since 1 = 1(1), k =1 and we see that for all values of x, y = x. So, completing the table we have:

x	1	1.5	2	2.5	3	3.5
y	3	4.5	6	7.5	9	10.5

3.   Estimates will vary. Possibility are:
   a.   x is about 10. 20 is one-fifth of 100 so x is one-fifth of 49. One-fifth of 49 is about 10.
        Exactly, x = (20/100)(49) = **9.8**.
   b.   Because 60 is half again as big as 40, x should be half again as big as 9. So x is 9 plus half of nine, about 13. Solving for x, x = (60/40)(9) = **13.5**.
   c.   As in b, 48 is about half again as big as 30. So x should be half again as big as 11, about 17. Solving, x = (11/30)(48) = **17.6**.

5.   Methods will vary. Possibilities include:
   a.   First, cross multiply to get: 20x + 40 = 70. Next, subtract 40 from both sides obtaining 20x = 30. Finally, divide both sides by 20 yielding **x = 1.5**.
   b.   Solving (3x/10) = 13/40 for x by multiplying each side by 10/3 gives **x = 13/12**.
   c.   The cross product gives 12x = 72. Dividing both sides of the equation by 12 produces **x = 6**.
   d.   Multiplying both sides of the proportion by 5 produces **x = (224/720)(5) = 14/9**.
   e.   First, cross products give 9x = 108 + 6x. Subtracting 6x from both sides produces 3x = 108. Dividing both sides by 3, we get **x = 36**.
   f.   The cross product produces 0.5x = 85. So **x = 170**.
   g.   First using the cross product and then dividing both sides by 2 we have: [3(344/144)]/2 = **x = 43/12**.
   h.   The cross product property produces 15x = 48. Dividing both sides by 15 gives **x = 48/15 = 16/5**.
   i.   The cross product gives 12 = 8x - 32.   Adding 32 and dividing by 8 we get **x = 5.5**.
   j.   The cross product gives 3x = 140 + 7x. Subtracting 7x and dividing by -4 produces **x = -35**.

7.   The lengths of corresponding sides of these rectangles do not vary proportionally because the length to length ratio is not equal to the corresponding width to width ratio. 10 to 5 is not equal to 20 to 15.

9.   Responses will vary. A possibility is: Let y = k x and let k = -2.

x	1	2	3	4	5	6
y	-2	-4	-6	-8	-10	-12

11.   Assuming that the rise and run are proportional we have: $7/12$ = rise/20. So rise = $(7/12)20$ = **11 2/3 ft**.

13.   Assuming proportionality: Copper : nickel = $3/1$ = $14/x$. So x = **14/3 or 4 2/3 lb nickel**.

15.   Methods of solving the proportion will vary. One possibility is: 6 cans : 1.80 = 24 cans : cost. Since the numerator 24 is 4 times the numerator 6, the cost associated with 24 cans is 4 times the $1.80 cost associated with 6 cans. So the cost is $4(1.80)$ = **$7.20**.

17.   Since 5 hours is 10 times 30 minutes, assuming proportionality, Laura would expect 10 times the commercial time. So 10(9 min) = **90 min or 1 ½ hours**.

19.   Reasoning will vary. a possibility is:

Days	1	2	3	4	5	6	7
Population	1	2	4	8	16	32	64

Since the ratio of population to day number is not constant the population **is not proportional** to the number of days.

21.   Reasons for disagreement will vary. One reason for **agreement** is that the ratio between all x,y pairs is constant.

23.   Responses will vary. A possibility is: Let M = $30,000 income and U = $300,000 income. U/M = 10/1. Now, the contributions are also in a 10/1 ratio. So the contributions **are proportional** to income and **Barbara is correct**.

25.   a. $2x/5$ = $8/17$ = 0.470588. So x = 5(.470588.)/2 = **1.176470588**.
       b.   Applying the reciprocal property we get: $5/2x$ = $17/8$ = 2.125. Now, $(2x)(2.125)$ = 5 and x = 5/ 4.25 = **20/17 = 1.176470588.....**.
       c.   With the calculator used for this example the answers are the same. However other calculators may truncate or round differently and produce slightly different answers.

27.   Responses will vary. The student, however, is **incorrect.** One may argue: Beginning with $3x/4$ = $5/7$, the calculator sequence first performs the computation $5 \div 7$, which is fine. This result, however, should be multiplied by 4 and that result divided by 3. The student has interchanged operations. By substituting the student's result into the left side expression we have 3(.5357)/4 = 0.4018 which is not equal to 5/7 = 0.714.

29.   Responses will vary. One solution is: They may divide the money in proportion to the number of hours each worked. So Dan get $40/(40 + 25 + 15)$ = ½ of the money. Shelly get 25/80 of the money and Kirby gets what is left. So **Dan gets $2000, Shelly gets $1250, and Kirby gets $750**.

31. Solutions will vary. One possibility is: If each of 30 persons is to drink 2 cans, then 60 cans are required. Now, 60 is 10 times 6. Since 6 cans costs $1.80 10 times 6 cans, 60 cans, will cost 10 times $1.80 or $18.00. So $20 **is sufficient money** for 60 cans.

33. Responses will vary. One set of possibilities is: Since x/3 = 7/9 we can multiply either side, or both sides, by the identity, 1, and the proportion will still be valid. There are an infinite number of rational numbers equivalent to 1: 2/2, 3/3, (8/7)/(8/7), and so on. Picking three of these we obtain the equivalent proportions: 2x/6 = 7/9, x/3 = 21/27, 3x/9 = 28/36.

35. Responses will vary. One possibility is: If the picture is 4 x 6 than frames with the same length to width ratio will have geometrically similar shapes and the picture will not have to be cropped. Two such frames would be 8 by 12 and 12 by 18. The square frame is not similar to the 4 by 6 picture and so the picture will have to be cropped to fit in a square frame.

37. Responses will vary. A possible argument is: The method will always work for proportions of the form a/x = b/c in which a, b, and c are non-zero numbers. After the first calculation Sang applied the reciprocal property to produce the valid proportion x/6 = 0.5. She then proceeded to solve for x by multiplying both sides of the proportion by 6. Substituting to confirm the answer we see that 6/3 is indeed equal to 14/7.

39. Given the equation $F = M V^2$, F is proportional to M provided V is a constant. If V is constant then V^2 is also a constant and F and M have the defining relation for quantities that are directly proportional, F = k M. To determine if F and V are proportional substitute some values. For convenience let M = 1. If V = 2 then F = 4 and if V = 3 then F = 9. Comparing the ratios of F to V we see that 4/2 < 9/3 and F and V are not proportional. Because V is squared it won't vary proportionally with F even if M is constant.

41. Responses will vary. Possibilities include: **Richie is correct.** Beginning with the proportion 8/5 = 20/x Richie obtained the equivalent proportion 1/5 = (20/8)/x = (2 1/2)/ x. He then applied the reciprocal property producing the still equivalent proportion 5/1 = x/(2 1/2) which he finally solved for x by multiplying both sides by 2 ½ yielding x = 12 1/2. **Martha's reasoning is also correct.** If 2 quantities are proportional then they are in a constant ratio. So let the ratio of a and b be a/b. Then a/b =2a / 2b = 3a / 3b = xa/xb = (x+1)a/(x+1)b. Now, the value of a halfway between xa and (x+1)a is a[(x + x + 1)]/2 = (x + 1/2)a and the value of b half way between xb and (x+1)b is (x + 1/2)b. The ratio between the 'halfway' values is a/b. So Martha, with a/b = 8/5, determined 2a/2b = 16/10 and 3a/3b = 24 to 15. The halfway value for the denominator is 16. The corresponding halfway value for the denominator is 12 1/2.

43. Responses will depend upon the extent to which the students have understood the concepts. Some of the concepts to include are: if the ratios of corresponding sides of two rectangles are equal, then the rectangles are similar in shape; if rectangles have the same area then the ratio of the lengths is the reciprocal of the ratio of the corresponding widths; the area of a rectangle varies proportionally to its width for a constant length.

45. Responses will vary. The square root of 5 is about 2.236067. This is approximated by the ratios: 22/10 = 2.2, 47/21 = 2.23809 is a better approximation, 85/38 = 2.23684 is better yet.

SECTION 7.3

1.

a.   b. 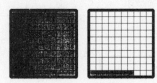   c.

d.    e.   f.

3.   60% = 0.6 So 0.6(20,000) = 12,000 students are accepted. 40% = 0.4. Thus 0.4(12,000) = **4800 students enroll**. Note that this could have been done: let E represent students enrolled.
Then E = (.6)(.4)(20,000) = 4 800.

5.   Let R represent the number of readers of the paper. Then we have (2%)R = 90, 0.02 R = 90,
R = 90/.02 = **4,500**.

7.   Since 25% = 0.25 the increase could be 0.25(17500) = $4375. So the total could be as much as
4375 + 17,500 =**$21,875** (and don't forget license, fees, taxes, and delivery charges).

9.   Let D represent the dollar discount, P the percent discount, and O the original price. Then D = (P/100) O.
So 25 = (20/100) O = O/5. So the original price was 5(25) = **$125**.

11. The percent increase was [(30,000 - 14,000)/14,000]100% = **114.29 %**.

13. Todd's percent loss was: [(190 - 220)/220]100% = -13.6 %. Cassidy's percent loss was: [(135-150)/150]100% = -10 %. So **Todd** had the greater percentage loss.

15. The use of the % key may vary among calculators. One possibility is to use the % key in place of the = key.
The % key performs 2 functions. It first divides the product by 100 and then displays the product.
a. **19.2**   b. **161.28**   c. **0.625**   d. **577.5**

17. Estimates will vary. The tip is about 15% of $40 which is about 1/10 of 40 plus half that amount or 4 + 2 =
$6.00. Essentially this is the reverse use of the distributive law: 15%(40) = [10% + 1/2(10%)] 40 =
(1/10)(40) + 1/2[(1/10)(40)].

19. Applying the same logic as in problem 17 we see that 1% of the number of bowlers is 1/100 of 725 or about 7
people. Another ½ percent is ½ of 7 or about 4 people. Thus we can expect about 7 + 4 = 11 out of the 725 to
bowl 200 or better.

21. The value of the stock will be **less** than the initial price. Arguments will vary. One possibility is: Let S
represent the initial price of the stock. Then after the 15% drop the stock is worth 85% S. Now, after the 15%
increase in price the value is 85%S + (15%)(85 % S) = 0.85 S + 0.1275 S = 0.9775 S which is less than S.

23. For simple interest, with r representing the yearly percentage interest, P the principle amount, t the time in years, and i the dollar amount of interest we have: i = Prt. So 4000 = 10,000 r (5) = 50,000 r. So r = 4000/50000 = **8%** simple interest.

25.

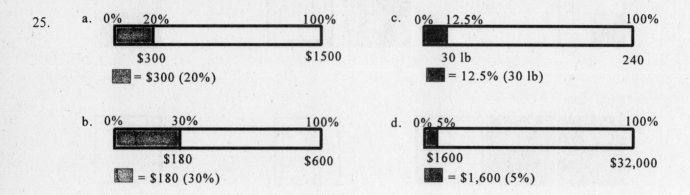

a. 0%   20%   100%
    $300 $1500
    = $300 (20%)

b. 0%   30%   100%
    $180 $600
    = $180 (30%)

c. 0%   12.5%   100%
    30 lb   240
    = 12.5% (30 lb)

d. 0% 5%   100%
    $1600 $32,000
    = $1,600 (5%)

27. The value, v, of an investment, p, with annual interest r compounded n times yearly for t years is:
v = p(1 + r/n)^{nt}. So v = 1000(1 + 0.08/365)$^{(365)1}$ = **$1083.28**. Since 1000(1 + 0.08328) = 1083.28 the simple interest would be **8.328 %**.

29. The value, v, of an investment, p, with annual interest r compounded n times yearly for t years is:
v = p(1 + r/n)^{nt}. Since compounding is yearly, n = 1, p = 1000, and v = 1000(1 + r)^{t}

	Yearly interest rates	6%	8%	12%
	Year			
a.	6	1419	1587	1974
b.	7	1504	1714	2211
c.	8	1594	1851	2476
d.	9	1689	1999	2773
e.	10	1791	2159	3106
f.	11	1898	2332	3479
g.	12	2012	2518	3896
h.	18	2854	3996	7690

31. One tenth of one percent of 350,600 is (.1/100)(350,600) = (1/1000)(350600), or about **351** people.

33. Inflation causes the purchasing power of money to decrease. So an inflation rate of 4% reduces the value of a dollar by 4% or reduces it to 96% of its previous value. So, from 1996 to 2000 we have 4 consecutive reductions of value of 4% or 4 consecutive revaluations of 96%. So the value of the $30 000 salary would be (.96)(.96)(.96)(.96)(30 000) = **$25,480.40**.

35. Suppose N represents the original number and P the percent decrease. The 5 % increase gives a value of 1.05N. Now we want to decrease this value by P % so that the new value (1 - P/100)(1.05N) = N. So we have (1 - P/100)(1.05) = 1; 1 - P/100 = 1/1.05; P = 100(1 - 1/1.05) = **4.76 %**.

37. Increasing a number by 100% means doubling the number. So to return to the original value the new value must be halved. Taking **50 %** of a number halves that number.

39. Suppose that Mark has 100 dollars to invest at 5% *simple* interest. Then he makes $5 per year. If the rate doubles to 10% then he makes $10 per year, double what he made at the lower rate. Now, Suppose Monica invests 100 at 5% *compounded* quarterly. Then in the first year she makes $100(1+.05/4)^4 = \$105.09$ If the rates double to 10% she makes $100(1 + 0.10/4)^4 = 110.38$ which is more than double her earnings at the lower interest rate. Mark is correct for simple interest, Monica for compound interest.

41. To arrive at a conjecture try some values for a and b. Because the order of multiplication does not affect the net raise we need not consider variations in order, first the smaller, then the larger and vice versa. It is good practice to consider three pairs for a and b: one in which the values are close, one in which they are equal, and one in which they are far apart. So first consider raises of 1% and 1 1/2%. The average is 1 1/4 %. For a $100 salary the separate raises would result in a salary of $100(1.01)(1.015) = \$102.515$. Applying the average twice we get $100(1.0125)(1.0125) = \$102.5156$. If the raises are equal, say 6%, the average is also 6% and the computations are the same. If the raises are quite different, say 1 % and 20% we have an average of 10.5%. The separate raises give a salary of $100(1.01)(1.20) = \$121.2$ and the average, twice applied, gives: 122.10, a more substantial raise.
So, **if the raises are not equal, the average twice applied give a greater raise.**

43. Responses will vary among students.

45. Suppose C represents the number of couples. Then $0.52 C - 0.39 C = 100$. So $0.13 C = 100$ and C is about **770 couples**.

CHAPTER 7 REVIEW EXERCISES

1 Responses will vary. Possibilities include:
a. A whole to part ratio is the ratio between all the students in the sixth grade class , S, and those students in the class who have a parent who speaks French at least occasionally, F. $S : F = 25 : 8$.
b. A part to part ratio is the ratio between F and those students in the class with parents who speak no French, N. This ratio is $F : N = 8 : 17$.
c. A part to whole ratio is the ratio between N and S. $N : S = 17 : 25$.

3. Converting to unit prices we have: a. $1.65 per 10 oz = 16.5 cents/oz; b. $1.50 per 9 oz = 16.7 cents/oz; c. $.96 per 6 oz = 16 cents/oz. So the order, best price to worst, is **c, a, b**.

5. Suppose the table is completed with values a, b, c, and d. Then $a/3 = b/4 = c/5 = d/6 = 2/5/2$. So a = 3.75, b = 5, c = 6.25, and d = 7.5

p	2	3	4	5	6
q	2.5	**3.75**	5	**6.25**	**7.5**

7. a. **True**. This is one of the definitions of proportional variation.
b. **False**. Suppose k = 4. Then if s = 2 r = 6 and if s = 4 r = 8. 2/6 is not equal to 4/8. So s and r are not proportional.
c. **False**. Let r = 8 and 8 = 4. Then r/s = 8/4 = 2/1. And (r+2)/(s+2) = 10/6 = 5/3. Since 2/1 is not equal to 5/3, this counter example shows that, in general r/s is not equal to (r+2)/(s+2).
d. **True**. This is the fundamental law of fractions and the numerators and denominators of equivalent representations of the same numbers are proportional.

9. a. $(x - 2)/12 = 5/6$; $(x - 2)/12 = 10/12$; so $(x-2) = 10$ and $x = 12$.
    b. $0.4/5 = x/7.5$; $5x = (0.4)(7.5) = 3$; $x = 0.6$.
    c. $15/4 = 45/x$; $15x = 4(45)$; $x = 12$.
    d. $4/x = 21/56$; $21x = 4(56)$; $x = 10\ 2/3$.

11. $12 : \$28 = 3 : x$. So $x = \$28/4 = \$7.00$.

13.

Percent	Decimal	Fraction
1/4 %	0.0025	1/400
150%	1.50	3/2
9.5%	0.095	19/299

15. Let S represent seatbelt users. Then $0.87(1700) = S = 1479$.

17. The percent decrease is: $(29{,}500 - 22{,}000)/29{,}500 = 25.4\ \%$.

19. Interest = principle times rate times time. So interest = $(\$2200)(.055)(2) = \$242$.

21. The methods of estimation and the estimates will vary. One possibility is: The room cost for 2 nights is $170. Together the taxes are 18%. Overestimate the taxes as 20% and underestimate the room cost as $150 dollars and the tax is estimated as $30. Add this to the actual room cost and the total comes to about $200.

23. Of the 1000 people contacted 500 were men and 500 women. Half the men, 250, said the would use the product. One fifth of the women, 100, said they would use the product. Thus **150** more men than women said they would use the product.

25. Of the initial 600 people 3 of 5 or 60% will respond. So 360 respond, 240 do not. Of the 240 one of three respond on the second mailing. Thus an additional 80 people respond leaving 160 who did not respond on either the first or second mailing. Of these, one in 8, or 20, can be expected to respond on a third mailing. So of the 600, **460** can be expected to respond over 3 mailings.

27. 1% of $a = (1/1000)a = a/1000$. 200.5% of $b = (200.5/100)b = 2005b/1000 = 401b/200$.

29. Since the value, v, of an investment, p, with annual interest r compounded n times yearly for t years is: $v = p(1 + r/n)^{nt}$, with a rate of 5% compounded daily and for a time of 1 year, some principle p would have a value of $v = p(1 + 0.05/365)^{1(365)} = p(1.0513)$. Since for simple interest we have $v = pit$ and the time is 1 year, the simple interest equivalent is **5.13 %**.

31. Discussions will vary. A 1 by 10 grid would serve as a model rather than our 10 by 10 grid. 0.5% would be 0.5/10 and 5% would be 5/10. A five percent increase would be half again as much. A 50% increase would mean five times as much as the original.

SECTION 8.1

1. A| ••••••••••
    B| •••••••••
    C| •••••••
    D| •••
    F| •

3.

Grade Distributions

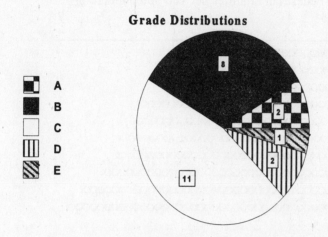

4. A
    B
    C
    D
    E

5.

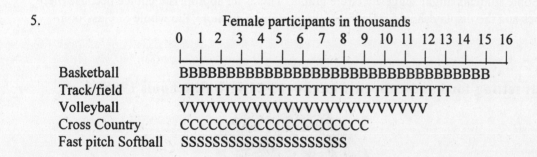

Female participants in thousands

| | 0 | 1 | 2 | 3 | 4 | 5 | 6 | 7 | 8 | 9 | 10 | 11 | 12 | 13 | 14 | 15 | 16 |

Basketball   BBBBBBBBBBBBBBBBBBBBBBBBBBBBBBBBBBBBBBBB
Track/field   TTTTTTTTTTTTTTTTTTTTTTTTTTTTTTTTTTTTT
Volleyball   VVVVVVVVVVVVVVVVVVVVVVVVVVVV
Cross Country   CCCCCCCCCCCCCCCCCCCCCCC
Fast pitch Softball SSSSSSSSSSSSSSSSSSSSSSS

7. a.

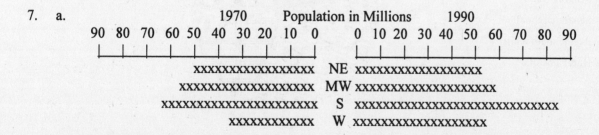

1970   Population in Millions   1990

90 80 70 60 50 40 30 20 10 0   0 10 20 30 40 50 60 70 80 90

        xxxxxxxxxxxxxxxxx NE xxxxxxxxxxxxxxxxx
        xxxxxxxxxxxxxxxxxx MW xxxxxxxxxxxxxxxxxxx
        xxxxxxxxxxxxxxxxxxxx S xxxxxxxxxxxxxxxxxxxxxxxxx
        xxxxxxxxxxx W xxxxxxxxxxxxxxxxx

    b. The **South** grew most rapidly, an average of 1.13 million persons per year.

9.   a.   Model years of cars on Sam's lot
         197| 5 6 8 9 9
         198| 2 2 3 4 5 6 6 7 9
         199| 0 0 1 2 2 2   197| 5 represents a car of model year 1975

     b.   The range of data is **17 years**, from 1975 to 1992.
     c.   The most common model year is **1992** with three vehicles made in that year.

11. Responses will vary. Students may selects a bar graph because the categories are non-numeric. A possible
     graph is:

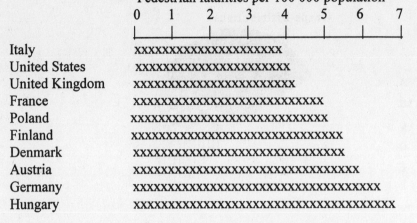

Pedestrian fatalities per 100 000 population

```
              0    1    2    3    4    5    6    7
              |    |    |    |    |    |    |    |

Italy         xxxxxxxxxxxxxxxxxxxxx
United States xxxxxxxxxxxxxxxxxxxxxx
United Kingdom xxxxxxxxxxxxxxxxxxxxxxx
France        xxxxxxxxxxxxxxxxxxxxxxxxx
Poland        xxxxxxxxxxxxxxxxxxxxxxxxx
Finland       xxxxxxxxxxxxxxxxxxxxxxxxxxx
Denmark       xxxxxxxxxxxxxxxxxxxxxxxxxxx
Austria       xxxxxxxxxxxxxxxxxxxxxxxxxxxxx
Germany       xxxxxxxxxxxxxxxxxxxxxxxxxxxxxx
Hungary       xxxxxxxxxxxxxxxxxxxxxxxxxxxxxxxxxx
```

13. Responses will vary. Some students might suggest a circle graph. This is an appropriate choice because there
     are only a few categories and the display should reflect the distribution of a whole, the whole of classroom
     settings.

Educational setting for handicapped students 18-21 in U.S. schools 1988

Regular class
Resource room
Separate class
Separate school
Residential facility
Home/hospital

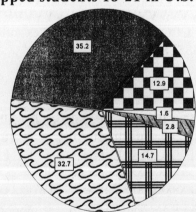

15. Responses will vary. Because of the number of categories, a bar graph is appropriate. A representative graph is:

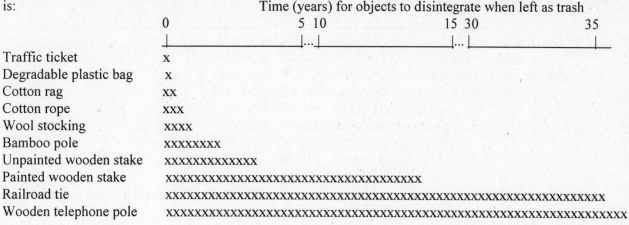

Time (years) for objects to disintegrate when left as trash

	0	5 10	15 30	35
Traffic ticket	x			
Degradable plastic bag	x			
Cotton rag	xx			
Cotton rope	xxx			
Wool stocking	xxxx			
Bamboo pole	xxxxxxxx			
Unpainted wooden stake	xxxxxxxxxxxx			
Painted wooden stake	xxxxxxxxxxxxxxxxxxxxxxxxxxxxxxxxxxxx			
Railroad tie	xxxxxxxxxxxxxxxxxxxxxxxxxxxxxxxxxxxxxxxxxxxxxxxxxxxxxxxxxxxxxxx			
Wooden telephone pole	xxxxxxxxxxxxxxxxxxxxxxxxxxxxxxxxxxxxxxxxxxxxxxxxxxxxxxxxxxxxxxxxxxx			

17. a. The **highest** was the **30-39** year old age group and the **lowest** was the **under 12** age group.
    b. Responses will vary.
    c. The percentage of AIDS deaths increases to age group 30-39 and then decreases.
    d. Responses will vary. A possibility is: The bar graph allows us to conclude that the percentage of deaths due to AIDS maximizes in the 30-39 year old age group

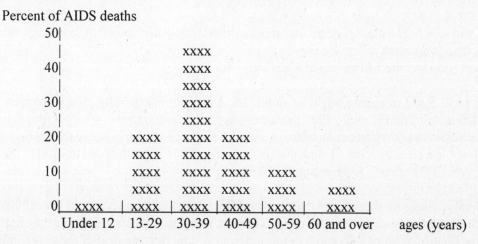

Percent of AIDS deaths

```
50|
  |                    xxxx
40|                    xxxx
  |                    xxxx
30|                    xxxx
  |                    xxxx
20|          xxxx   xxxx xxxx
  |          xxxx   xxxx xxxx
10|          xxxx   xxxx xxxx  xxxx
  |          xxxx   xxxx xxxx  xxxx        xxxx
 0|  xxxx  | xxxx | xxxx | xxxx | xxxx |   xxxx |
     Under 12  13-29  30-39   40-49  50-59 60 and over      ages (years)
```

19. a.

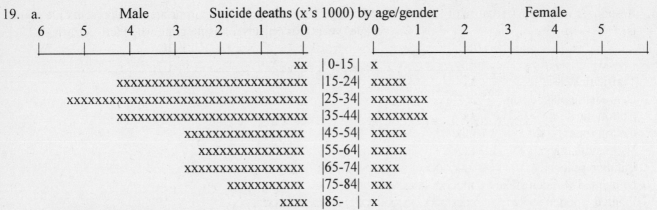

xx	| 0-15 |	x
xxxxxxxxxxxxxxxxxxxxxxxxxxxx	|15-24|	xxxxx
xxxxxxxxxxxxxxxxxxxxxxxxxxxxxxxxxx	|25-34|	xxxxxxxx
xxxxxxxxxxxxxxxxxxxxxxxx	|35-44|	xxxxxxxx
xxxxxxxxxxxxxxxx	|45-54|	xxxxx
xxxxxxxxxxxxxx	|55-64|	xxxxx
xxxxxxxxxxxxxxxx	|65-74|	xxxx
xxxxxxxxxxx	|75-84|	xxx
xxxx	|85- |	x

b. The data distribution is similar for both genders. The distributions have maxima closer to the low values than to the high values.

c. Responses will vary. The may include the observations that the number of suicides for males is far greater than the number for females at any age. Both genders have the maximum number of suicides in early adulthood.

21. a.   Class A scores   Class B

        1 0 0 |14| 0 1 1 1 2 |14| 0 represents a score of 140
     5 5 2 1 0 0 |13| 0 0 1 2 25 7 8
     9 8 7 6 5 0 |12| 1 6 7 8
         9 8 5 |11| 8

b. Responses will vary.   The class A scores are more symmetrically distributed. Class B has relatively more high scores than low scores.

c. The 3 class A scores in the 140's constitute a cluster.

23. Responses will vary. Some responses might be similar to: A dot plot is generally used when specific values are repeated. A frequency plot is used when the values are placed in categories. The dot plot is used for, generally, fewer values than the frequency table. A dot plot might be used to display the scores on a quiz of, perhaps, 10 points for a class of 15 to 30 students. A frequency table might be used to display the scores of a lecture class, maybe 200 students, on an exam of 200 points.

25. Responses will vary. Students should note that Standard Oil controlled the majority of the oil industry resources at either end: raw materials and storage. Although Standard oil controlled less than half of the refining capacity, control of input and output to refineries gave it de facto control of the entire industry.

SECTION 8.2

1. Responses may vary.   A possibility: After a large drop in potential increases in employer healthcare costs in 1994, they have risen until a scant four years later these potential increases exceed those of 1993.

3.

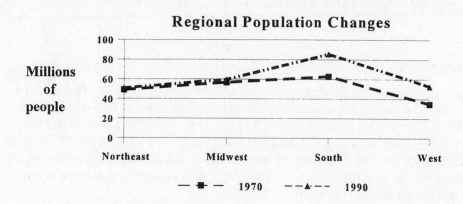

5. Responses will vary. Among the conclusions students may note are: Domestic consumption of plywood and veneer has grown only slightly between 1970 and 1990. Although subject to major fluctuations, domestic consumption of lumber has increased some 30% in the 20 years. After flat usage from 1970 to 1977, fuel wood showed a large and rapid growth until 1980 and only slight growth thereafter.

7. (a) shows no correlation between the variables. (b) shows a relatively strong positive correlation and (d) a relatively weak positive correlation. (c) shows a relatively weak negative correlation.

9. Responses will vary. (b), with the long vertical axis, emphasizes small changes in the vertical variable.

11. No, the trend line would not be appropriated to give an expected class average for an ACT of 34. The graph does not continue linearly because there are maxima to both ACT and class average. The extension of the trend line gives a class average greater than 100 for an ACT score of 34.

13. a. There is a positive correlation between the variables.   In general, an increase in the value of one variable is accompanied by an increase in the value of the other variable.
    b. By reducing the separation of the points on the vertical axis the correlation could be made to appear stronger. This could be done by increasing the maximum value of the window in the vertical direction from 60 to, perhaps, 100.

15. Responses will vary. One approach is: Because the emphasis is on the growth of population, not the actual population figures, the data will be best represented with a bar graph.

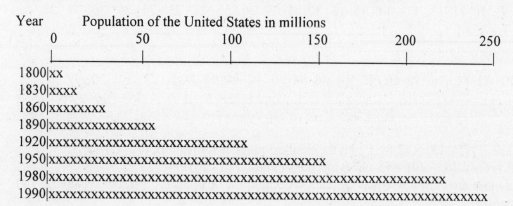

17.   Responses will vary with the research of the students.

SECTION 8.3

1.   Before performing computations, order those data sets that are not initially ordered. The sum of each set is in
     parentheses after the set. The middle value, or the middle pair, of each data set is underlined.
        0 0 1 2 2 4 5 10 (24)   6 7 8 9 10 12 15 15 20 28 (130)   72 80 80 82 88 90 96 (588)
     61 68 68 73 85 91 93 (539)   68 74 80 82 83 85 86 88 91 93 (830)   -15 -2 -1 0 0 7 7 8 14 (18)
     To determine the mean divide the sum of the data by the number of values. The median is either the middle
     value of the mean of the middle pair, the mode is the most frequently occurring value, and the midrange is the
     mean of the highest and lowest values.

	mean	median	mode	midrange
a.	3	2	0,2	5
b.	13	11	15	17
c.	84	82	80	84
d.	77	73	68	77
e.	83	84	None	80.5
f.	2	0	0,7	-0.5

3.   a.   The mean score is (75 + 80 + 80 + 85)/4 = 80. Since 80 occurs more frequently than any other score it is
          the mode. The median is the mean of the two middle score, also 80. So the **mean, median, and mode
          are all 80**.
     b.   Because mean, median, and mode are all equal, the "average" used is irrelevant.
     c.   If the mean is to be 84, then representing the fifth score by s we would have: (75+80+80+85+s)/5 = 84.
          So, 320 + s = 420, s = **100**. Based on Doug's previous performance, a score of 100 is unlikely.

5.   a.

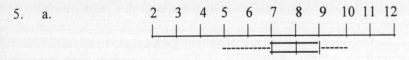

     b.

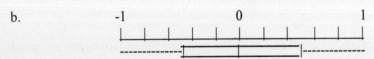

     c.

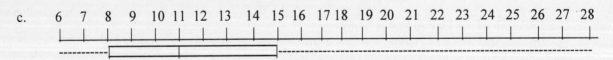

     d.

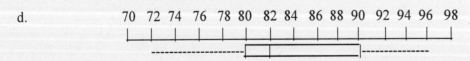

7.   a.   The greatest range is (95 - 13) = 82 for C and the smallest range is for team B, (72 - 5) = 67.
     b.   The largest IQR is for C (85 - 40) = 45 and B has the smallest, (48 - 30) = 18.
     c.   The median and mean are closest to equal for team B because the box plot is closest to symmetric with
          respect to the median.
     d.   The mean is most likely to exceed the median for team A because the scores above the median are
          generally farther from the median that are the scores below the median.

9.   Since the range of the data is the difference between the highest and lowest of the data values, the range is (57 - 29) = 28.

11. The range is the difference between the highest and lowest scores. So the range is (98 - 55) = 43. The mean is the sum of all scores divided by the number of scores. The mean is (55+67+80+85+90+92+98)/7 = 81. A data set with the same mean but smaller range is {78,79,80,81,82,83,84}. The range of this set is 6. Note that the data in pairs (78,84), (79,83), (80,82) have means of 81 and the single unpaired value is 81.

13. Helen bought 10 items for a total cost of 3(0.47) + 5(0.71) + 2(1.21) = $7.38. So the average cost was $7.38/10: **$0.738 or 73.8 cents**.

15. a. Responses will vary. Students may note that the overall scoring is very similar. Comparing the Flyers' range and average to those of the Bombers we have 763 to 758 and 2156 to 2158.
     b. To determine which team is more likely to win a game we determine the points per game (ppg) averages for each of the players. For the Flyers we have: 31.46, 29.05, 28.39, 27.60, and 26.59. These 5 Flyers together average 143 ppg. The Bombers have 31.60, 29.80, 28.2, 23.29, and 26.4: a combined ppg of 139. Thus the Flyers are more likely to win the game.

17. **NO**, the standard deviation is not always less than the variance. Suppose that the variance is a number between 0 and 1. Then the square root of the variance, the standard deviation is greater than the variance. For example, suppose the variance were 0.81. Then the standard deviation would be 0.9.

19. Suppose that the original data are a, b, c, and d. Then the mean is (a+b+c+d)/4. Now, if 10 points are added to each of the scores, then the mean becomes (a+10 + b+10 + c+10 + d+10)/4 = (a + b + c + d)/4 + 10. So the mean has increased by 10 points. Because the mode is one (or more) of the data points, adding 10 points to each value would increase the mode by 10 points. If the median is one of the data (there are an odd number of points) then the median would be increased by 10 points because all data are increased by 10 points. If there are an even number of data, then the median is a mean of 2 points and, as in the case of the overall mean, would increase by 10 points. The standard deviation is calculated from the differences between each value and the mean. Since each of these is increased by 10 points the differences are unaffected and the standard deviation is not affected by the addition of the 10 points to each score.

21. The original data set, O, {0,12,13,15,17,17,18,20} becomes N = {5,12,13,15,17,17,18,25}. Because the mean is the sum of the data values divided by the number of values and since the sum has increased but the number of values has not, the mean will increase by 10/number of values. The median will not be affected because its determination does not involve H and L. Since neither H nor L is the mode, the mode will be unaffected. The midrange will increase by 5. The median of both sets of data is 16. The mode of both sets is 17. The midrange of O is (0+20)/2 = 10, the midrange of N is (5 + 25)/2 = 15. The mean of O is 14, of N, 15.25.

23. The mean, median, and midrange need not be members of the data set that they describe. The are calculated from members of the data set. The median is always a member of the set for an odd number of data. The mode is always a member of the data set because it is that member of the data most frequently occurring.

25. Responses will vary depending upon the definition of 'middle' of a data set. Some students may chose the median and argue that the middle is more related to the number of data than to the values of the data. Others may use the 'balance point' idea and chose the mean as the best representative of middle.

27. Responses will vary depending upon the research of the students.

29. Responses will vary among students. They may discuss that variance and the related standard deviation have most meaning for normally distributed data. The standard deviation is related to the probabilities of outcomes in some defined range of the possible outcomes. These relations are of interest to those who participate in games of chance. Initially they may help one determine if a game is 'worth' playing.

SECTION 8.4

1. Responses will vary. Some considerations are:
   a. The statement does not describe either the characteristics of the sample of persons responding or the criteria upon which they were to make judgements of the greatest American jazz musician.
   b. This argument involves an unwarranted causation. Plato, St. Augustine, St. Thomas Aquinas, Hobbes, and Descartes may very well be unmarried philosophers but the lack of a spouse may be only coincidentally related to their pursuits.
   c. The sample of persons surveyed may very well not be representative of the snacking American population. Further, they may have been responding to a perceived question: "What is your favorite snack at a ball game?".
   d. There are at least 2 difficulties here: one, the persons flying to Normal Illinois may not be representative of the flying population and second, the choices of carriers into Normal isn't representative of the population of air carriers.
   e. There are many levels of professional baseball, class D through the majors. The statements does not define the population of player to which the conclusion is to be applied.
   f. The ad does not specify the criteria for measuring cleanliness nor does it state twice as clean as what?

3. Most people use either angles or arc lengths to compare the amounts represented by pie charts. The 3-D perspective of this pie chart distorts both of these common measures. The 26% share appears to have the an angle and arc length greater than the 30% share. It would be better to use a non-perspective pie chart for this presentation.

5. The claim is correct. At least one poultry dog has about 170 calories and at least one beef dog has about 110 calories. The product of 1.5 and 110 is less than 170. However, the graphs also show that almost three quarters of all poultry dogs have fewer calories that do three quarters of all meat and beef dogs. The graphs show that if a product is picked at random, one is more likely to get fewer calories in a poultry dog than in a beef or meat dog. Judicious selection of meat or beef dogs can result in a rather low calorie item.

7. Responses will vary among students. Not only has minority enrollment significantly increased in absolute terms, it has also significantly increased as a percentage of total college enrollment. The continuing trends for both of these measures suggest continued increases.

9. Responses will vary. The general implication is negative. The cartoon implies that even though the level of performance remains the same, a statistician will be able to make the team appear more competent.

CHAPTER 8 REVIEW EXERCISES

1. To deal with the data set, first make the plots. The S/L and dot plots are ordering techniques and ordered data
    is required to produce the box plot.

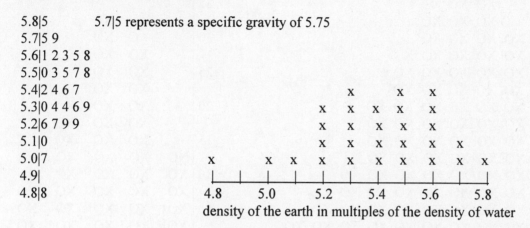

```
5.8|5          5.7|5 represents a specific gravity of 5.75
5.7|5 9
5.6|1 2 3 5 8
5.5|0 3 5 7 8
5.4|2 4 6 7
5.3|0 4 4 6 9
5.2|6 7 9 9
5.1|0
5.0|7
4.9|
4.8|8
```

density of the earth in multiples of the density of water

There are 29 data points. The sum of the data values is 157.99. So the mean is 5.4479 and the range is
(5.85 - 4.88): 0.97. The median is the 15th value counting from top or bottom, 5.46 and the modes are   5.34
and 5.29 each repeating twice. Q1 is the mean of the 7th and 8th values counting from the least,
(5.29 + 5.30)/2 = 5.295 and Q3 is the mean of the 7th and 8th values counting down from the top:
(5.62 + 5.61)/2 = 5.615. We can now produce the box and whisker plot

density of the earth as a multiple of the density of water

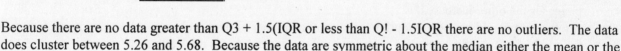

Because there are no data greater than Q3 + 1.5(IQR or less than Q! - 1.5IQR there are no outliers. The data
does cluster between 5.26 and 5.68. Because the data are symmetric about the median either the mean or the
median is a good representation of the density of the earth: about 5.4.

3.

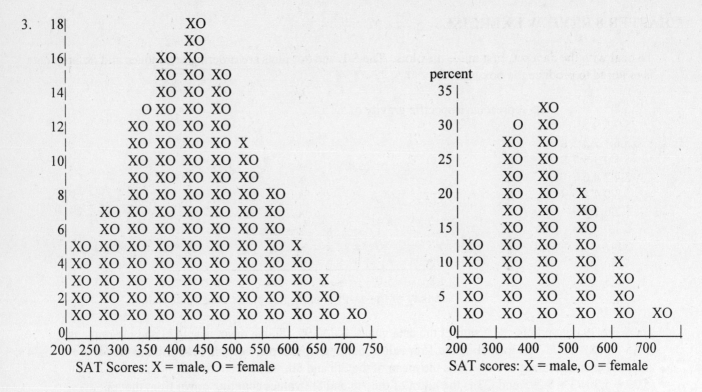

SAT Scores: X = male, O = female

SAT scores: X = male, O = female

Both graphs show a slightly higher percentage of males with scores in the higher ranges.

5. a. The data set for 'Sightings Confirmed' is {2,2,3,3,4,5,5,8,9,10,12,13,13,14,16} and for 'Reported Sightings' is {2,3,3,3,4,5,6,9,10,11,13,15,15,16,19}. Because there are 15 data values in each set the median values are the 8th counting from lowest: **8 Confirmed Sightings and 9 Reported Sightings**.

b. The graph suggests a **positive correlation** between reported and confirmed sightings because as one increases the other increases.

c. A trend line would not be appropriate because the number of data is close to the tornado population for for any May. Extending the data to larger numbers of tornados is misleading.

7. The conclusion on the city's "best" restaurant is not valid. The criteria for best is not defined. The crowd at a ball game may not be a sample representative of the population as a whole and the first 50 may be snack bar aficionados who planned to eat at the snack bar because they consider that to be fine dinning.

9.

Aluminum Bat Distances (ft)		Wooden Bat Distances (ft)
7 4	|17|	
7 7 0	|16|	3
6 1	|15|	1 3 4 6 9
9 7 2	|14|	2 7
9 0	|13|	9
3	|12|	1 3 7 7
5	|11|	7
5	|10|	
	|9|	|14| 2 represents 142 ft
	|8|	6

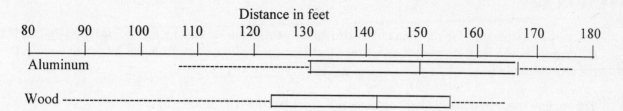

Distance in feet

Arguments will vary. They may include the concepts that the aluminum bat provided more consistent as well as greater distance hitting.

11.
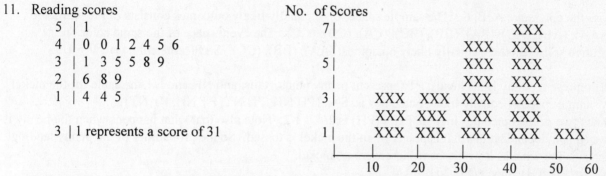

Reading scores	
5	1
4	0 0 1 2 4 5 6
3	1 3 5 5 8 9
2	6 8 9
1	4 4 5

3 | 1 represents a score of 31

Responses will vary. The histogram conveys the primary information, distribution of, and general values of, the reading scores in a more emphatic manner.

13. Responses will vary among students. Samples should be drawn randomly.

15. Responses will vary. The may be similar to: The last graph has 40 data points. But there are are 20 students so this graph cannot display the (student/pockets) data from the class. Turn graphs 1 and 2 sideways to get a more conventional view of a dot plot. Thus we see that the second graph represents the data because the first graph show 10 students with no pockets and we are assured that most of the students do have pockets.

17. Responses will vary. Students should be wary of using the means of the first 6 and the last 6 races to compare performances because of the unusually large value for the 10th race.

SECTION 9.1

1. Since every element of the set {m,a,t,h} is also an element of the set {ma,t,h,e,i,c,s}, it is <u>certain</u> that if an element is chosen from the set {m,a,t,h,} then that element is also chosen from the set {m,a,t,h,e,i,c,s}. Thus the probability is **1**.

3. The sample space of equally likely outcomes, S, for a fair die is {1,2,3,4,5,6}.
    a. For event E = {5,6}, P(E) = 2/6 = **1/3**.
    b. For event E = {1,3,5}, P(E) = 3/6 = **1/2**
    c. For event E = {1,2,3,4,5}, P(E) = **5/6**.
    d. For event E = {2,3,4,6}, P(E) = 4/6 = **2/3**.

5. Suppose the colors are A, B, C. The sample space, S, of equally likely outcomes consists of the 9 ordered pairs (AA), (AB), (AC), (BA), (BB), (BC), (CA), (CB), (CC). The event space of the same color on consecutive spins has three equally likely outcomes: (AA), (BB), (CC). So P(same color) = 3/9 = **1/3**.

7. Let PH represent penny lands heads, PT represent penny lands tails, and NH and NT the same for the nickel.
    a   A sample space of equally likely outcomes is S = {PH NH, PH NT, PT NH, PT NT}.
    b. Since two of the outcomes include PH, P(PH) is 2/4 = **1/2**. Note also that what happens when the penny is tossed is independent of what happens when the nickel is tossed. So the probability of the penny landing heads is the same as it would be if there were no nickel.
    c. If E = {PH NH}, then P(PH NH) = **1/4**.
    d. The event both coins don't match is E = {PH NT, PT NH}. P(E) = 2/4 = **1/2**.

9. Completing the table we see that there are 386 males, 405 females, 201 Freshmen, 198 Sophomores, 200 juniors, and 192 seniors, and 791 total students.
    a. P(male) = **386/791 or about 0.488**.
    b. P(sophomore) = **198/791 or about 0.250**.
    c. P(male given sophomore) = **97/198 or about 0.49**.
    d. P(junior or senior given female) = (105+101)/(98+101+105+101) = **206/405 or about 0.509**.

11. P(A) = 1/5 and P(B) = 1/5. So P(A or B) = 1/5 + 1/5 = **2/5**.

13. The sample space of equally like outcomes is the last 42 attempts. The event success has 34 elements. So P(success) = 34/42. Thus the probability of the next free throw being successful, assuming the attempt is under comparable conditions, is **34/42**: about 0.81.

15. The uniform sample space, S, with M = male and F = female, is S = {MM, MF, FM, FF}.
    a. P(MM) = **1/4**.   c. P(no girls) = P(MM) = **1/4**.
    b. P(FM) = **1/4**.   d. P(at least one girl) = P(MF or FM or FF) = **3/4**.

17. A uniform sample space for 2 coin flips is {HH, HT, TH, TT}. So P(P(no heads) = P(TT) = **1/4**.

19. The average output of A is (2/7)1 + (3/7)3 + (2/7)5 = 3; of B, 24/9 = 2 2/3; of C, 2. Assuming the same input to each machine per play, A has the greatest output whether the player is alone or with company. So chose A in either case.

21. The uniform sample space, S, for the 12-sided die could be {1,1,2,2,3,3,4,4,5,5,6,6} producing P(1) = 2/12 or 1/6. P(2), P(3), P(4), P(5), and P(6) are also 1/6, the same as on a common 6-side die.

23. On the first roll of the die any of the six numbers may come up. But on the second roll only five of the numbers will prevent duplication. And on the third roll only four of the numbers will prevent duplication. Finally, on the sixth roll only a single number will permit each number showing once. Thus there are (6)(5)(4)(3)(2)(1) = 720 different sequences of six throws yielding each number once. But there are (6)(6)(6)(6)(6)(6) = 46656 possible sequences for the six throws. Thus P(each number once) = **720/46656 or approximately 0.01543**.

25. P(H Leclerc) = 2048/4040 = **0.5069**. P(H Pearson) = 12012/24000 = **0.5005**. Theoretical probability estimates improve with larger sample sizes, so it appears that a better estimate would be obtained by a combination of the data. P(H combined data) = 14060/28040 = **0.5014**. There is an apparent anomaly here. If we believe that the 'real' probability of heads is 1/2, then adding Pearson on top of Leclerc seems to help while adding the Leclerc data on top of the Pearson data appears to hurt. Because Leclerc and Pearson were conducting different experiments, different coins, the data should not be combined. Leclerc's experiments estimate the theoretical probability associated with his coin, Pearson's experiments with *his* coin.

SECTION 9.2

1. Any one of the three letters may be placed in the first position. But for each of these only 2 letters may be placed in the second position. For each of the six of the placements of the first two letters only 1 letter may be placed in the third position. Thus there are (3)(2)(1) = **6** different code symbols. These are: SPY, SYP, PSY, PYS, YSP, YPS.

3. For each of the six tops there are four bottoms. And for each of these 24 top/bottom combinations the child can select from five pairs of shoes. So there are (6)(4)(5) = **120** different outfits.

5. We know that the first card drawn was a king and that this card is not to be replaced. So the deck now contains 51 cards, 3 of which are kings. The probability of drawing one of these kings is **3/51**. Because we know that the first card drawn was a king, the probability of drawing 2 kings is just the probability of getting a king on the second draw.

7. The sample space for selecting a number from the set of natural numbers 1 through 9 is {1,2,3,4,5,6,7,8,9}. But if we know that the number selected is prime it is certain that the number selected is in the set {2,3,5,7}. Of the 4 equally likely outcomes in this restricted sample space, 3 are odd. So the probability of selecting a odd number, knowing that it is prime, is **3/4, or 0.75**.

9. If the sum is to be eight and one die shows 5, then the other die must show 3. Now, the entire sample space for 2 dice has 36 equally likely outcomes:

	1	2	3	4	5	6			1	2	3	4	5	6	
1								1					x		The x's indicate the restricted sample
2		unrestricted						2					x		space based on the information that one of
3		sample space for						3					x		the dice shows 5. It has 11 equally likely
4		tossing 2 dice:						4					x		outcomes.
5		36 equally likely						5	x	x	x	x	x	x	
6		outcomes						6					x		

In the restricted sample space there are 2 successes, threes. So the probability of an 8 given one die with a 5 is **2/11**.

11. The table of data could be enhanced:

	No Help	Help	Total
Drug	22	47	69
Placebo	31	20	51
Total	53	67	120

    a. Since 69 persons received the drug and 47 perceived that it helped, the probability is **47/69**.

    b. The probability that a person receiving a placebo perceived that it helped is **20/51**.

    c. The probability that a subject perceived that he/she was helped is **67/120**.

13. The important characteristic is the area of the various circles:

Radius	Area
2	12.56
4	50.24
6	113.04
8	200.96
10	314.00

    a. The sample space is 200.96 sq in and the event is 12.56 sq in. So the probability is 12.56/200.96 = **0.0625**.

    b. The probability of the dart hitting the 2 inch circle given that it is in the 6 inch circle is 12.56/113.04 = **0.11**.

    c. The probability of the dart hitting the 2 inch circle given that it is in the 4 inch circle is 12.56/ 50.24 = **0.25**.

    d. The probability of the dart hitting the 2 inch circle given that it is in the 2 inch circle is 12.56/ 12.56 = **1**.

15. The probability of getting any single question correct is 1/2.

    a. On a 4 item test the probability of getting question 1 correct and question 2 correct and question 3 correct and question 4 correct is (1/2)(1/2)(1/2)(1/2) = **1/16**.

    b. The probability of getting all 10 questions correct on a ten item test is $(1/2)^{10}$ = **1/1024**.

17. a. The first draw can be a card of either color. Half of the second draws will match the first color, half won't. So the probability of drawing two cards of the same color is the probability of a match on the second draw: **1/2**.

    b. Reasoning as in (a), the first draw will produce a card of some suit. After that card is replaced, one fourth of the cards are of that suit. So the probability of matching the suit of the first card drawn on the second draw is 1/4. So there is a probability of **1/4** that both cards will be from the same suit.

    c. If the draws are made without replacement then the probability of the results of the second draw are different from parts (a) and (b). The probability of matching the color of the first card drawn is **25/51, approximately 0.49** and the probability of matching the suit of the first card drawn is **12/51, about 0.24**.

19. The pairings might look like:

Thus there would have to be **19** games.

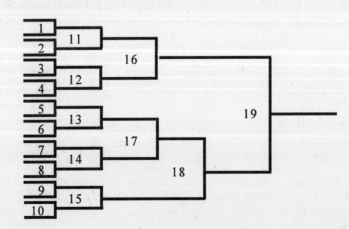

21. In order to obtain a total of 20, given that the first throw was a 2, the second two throws must each be 9. Now, there are four 9's on the 25 square board. So the probability of getting a 9 on any one throw is 4/25. Thus the probability of getting 2 consecutive 9's is (4/25)(4/25) = **16/625**.

23. The complimentary event to throwing neither A nor B is to throw either A or B (or both)   Since the probability of throwing neither is 3/9 the probability of the complimentary event is 1 - 3/9 = **6/9**.

25. To win the game the shooter must make both the first shot and the second. The probability of this happening is (0.6)(0.6) = **0.36**. To tie the game the shooter must make the first and miss the second. Since make and miss are complementary events, the probability of missing is 0.4. So the probability of a tie is (0.6)(0.4) = **0.24**.

27. The $2 should be distributed in the same ratio as the probabilities of each player winning the game were it to be played to completion. The tree diagram show that the probability of A winning on the first or second toss is ½ + 1/4 = 3/4 and the probability of B winning is 1/4. So the $2 should be split $1.50 to A, $0.50 to B, a ratio of 3/1.

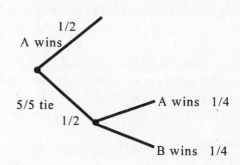

SECTION 9.3

1. There are several approaches to this problem. Theoretically, there are 2 possibilities for the first child, 2 for the second, 2 for the third, and 2 for the fourth: a total of 16 arrangements of gender from BBBB to GGGG. Of these 16, 4 have 3 boys: BBBG, BBGB, BGBB, GBBB. So the probability of three boys and a girl is **4/16, or 1/4**. A second approach is to simulate the birth of 4 children by, say, tossing four coins and letting heads represent the birth of a boy, tails the birth of a girl. one hundred trials of this experiment produced the results:

Number of heads	number of trials
0	3
1	26
2	45
3	24
4	2

Thus the simulated probability of 3 boys out of four children is 0.24.

3. Theoretically, since making and missing free throws are complementary events, the probability of missing a free throw is 0.75.   The probability of missing both the first and the second of a pair of free throws is (0.75)(0.75) = **0.5625**. This can be simulated by selecting 100 groups of 4 random numbers. Let the first 2 of each group of 4 random numbers represent the front end of a pair of free throws and the second 2 numbers represent the second shot. Numbers 00 through 24 represent success in making the free throw, 25 through 99 represents missing. For example 7256 means the player missed both shots and 2181 represents making the first and missing the second.

5. Showing up and not showing up are complementary events. Since the probability of not showing up is 1/6, the probability of showing up is 5/6. So the probability of 7 persons showing up is $(5/6)^7$ = **0.279**.

7. A possible experiment is flipping a coin 3 times to represents the birth of 3 children: heads representing the birth of a boy, tails the birth of a girl. Repeating the experiment 50 times represents 50 families with 3 children. Sample results are:

Outcome	Frequency	Probability		Outcome	Frequency	Probability
HHH	14	0.14		HTT	8	0.08
HHT	15	0.15		THT	14	0.14
HTH	11	0.11		TTH	13	0.13
THH	12	0.12		TTT	13	0.13

Because there are 8 equally likely outcomes the theoretical probability of each is **0.125**.

9. Rand produces random numbers between 0 and 1. Six times Rand produces random numbers between 0 and 6 and Int(6xRand) produces integers between 0 and 5 inclusive. Thus Int(6xRand) + 1 produces the integers 1 to 6 inclusive.

11. To simulate the choice of a locker numbered from 1 to 1000 we must produce random numbers from 1 to 1000. The random number generator of a calculator produced random numbers between 0 and 1. So 1000xRand will produce random numbers between 0 and 999.99.... Int(1000xRand) produces the integers from 0 to 999 inclusive so **Int(1000xRand)+1** will yield the integers between 1 and 1000 inclusive.

13. This situation could be simulated by tossing a die. The numbers 1 and 2 represent toy 1, the numbers 3 and 4 represent toy 2, and the numbers 5 and 6 represent toy 3. Rolling the die one represents a meal. 5 rolls of the die represents one trial of getting five meals. For example, if in 5 rolls the numbers 1,3,4,3,6,5 were displayed then toys 1, 2, 2 ,2, and 3 would be awarded. Out of 100 trials of 5 meals, all 3 toys were awarded 73 times for a probability of 0.73.

15. To simulate the situation is which the probability of team A winning any one game is 0.7, select random one digit numbers. A selection of 0 through 6 indicates that A wins the game, 7,8,9 that B wins. A series is over when either A or B wins 4 games. Count the number of games in each series. Sample results are:

Games to win series	Frequency
7	8
6	12
5	15
4	15

The average number of games required to win the series is: [8(7) + 12(6) + 15(5) + 15(4)]/50 = 5 to the nearest whole game.

17. This could be simulated by, in each trial, rolling a pair of dice 6 times. Doubles on the dice correspond to a key correctly assigned to a car. Sample results are:

Number of matches	Frequency
0	38
1	35
2	19
3	7
4	1
0	0
0	0

Of the 100 trials at least one key was correctly assigned 62 times. So the probability is about 0.62.

19. a. P(green and green and green and green) = P(green) x P(green) x P(green) x P(green)
      = (0.4)(0.4)(0.4)(0.4) = **0.0256**.
   b. P(all are red) = P(red) x P(red) x P(red) x P(red) = (0.6)(0.6)(0.6)(0.6) = **0.1296**.
   c. At least one light red is the complement to all lights green and thus has a probability of 1 - 0.0256 = **0.9744**.
   d. The probability of the first light red and the last 2 green is (0.6)(0.4)(0.4) = **0.096**.

21. This could be simulated by taking 2 complete suits of cards, shuffling both thoroughly, dealing one suit and then dealing the other suit on top of the first. Then count matches. Sample results are:

Number of matches	Frequency
0	32
1	40
2	23
3	5
4 - 13	0

The average number of matches is [0(32) + 1(40) + 2(23) + 3(5)]/100 = **1 match per trial**.

SECTION 9.4

1. The odds in favor of drawing 2 spades on successive draws without replacement can be calculated as the quotient of the probability of drawing two spades and the probability of not drawing 2 spades. The various probabilities may be represented in a tree:

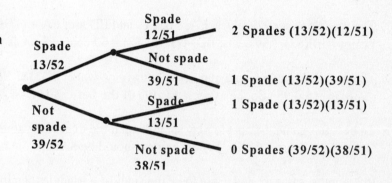

   So the odds are:
   [(13/52)(12/51)]/[(13/52)(39/51)
   + (39/52)(13/51) + (39/52)(38/51)]
   = **156/2496 = 0.0625**.

3. Of the 52 possible draws from a deck of cards only 4 result in drawing a king and 48 result in not drawing a king. The odds against drawing a king are **48:4**.

5. The odds, O, in favor of an event A are equal to P(A) / [1 - P(A)].
   a. O = (5/9) / (1 - 5/9) = **5/4**.
   b. O = (0.33...) / (1 - 0.333...) = **1/2**.
   c. O = (6/29) / (1 - 6/29) = **6/23**.

7. There are 36 equally likely outcomes for 2 consecutive tosses of 1 die.
   a. There are five outcomes that produce a sum of 6: (2,4), (4,2), (1,5), (5,1), (3,3). So there are 31 outcomes that will not produce a sum of 6. Therefore the odds in favor of a sum of 6 are **5/31**.
   b. The sums less than 4 are 2 and 3 and are in 3 outcomes: (1,1), (1,2), and (2,1). So there are 33 outcomes which will not produce sums less than 4. So the odds in favor of a sum less than 4 are **3/33**.
   c. Since all outcomes have sums that are greater than 1 the odds in favor of a sum greater than 1 are **36/0**.

9. a. Since there are 2 ways for a green number to show and 36 ways for a non-green number to come up the odd in favor of green are **2/36 = 1/18**.

    b. Of the 38 numbers 0, 00, 1, 2, 3, ..., 36 eleven are prime: 2, 3, 5, 7 ,11, 13, 17, 19, 23, 29, and 31. So the odd in favor of a prime number winning are **11/27**.

    c. Since 18 numbers are red. the odds in favor of a red number winning are **18/20 = 9/10**.

    d. Because 18 of the numbers are odd, the odds in favor of an odd number winning are **18/20 = 9/10**.

11. We can interpret the 0.4 probability of snow as of 10 weather events that may happen, 4 of them are snow, 6 are not snow. So the odd against it snowing (that is, the odds in favor of no snow) are **6/4 = 3/2**.

13. The expected gain, G, is the difference between premium and expected payout. G = 120 - 0.002(50,000) = **$20**.

15. P(BC) = 1/26 and P(D) = 1/51. So, assuming the diseases are independent, P(BC and D) = (1/26)(1/51) = 1/1326. So the odds that a woman will develop both diseases are: (1/1326) / [1 - (1/1326)] = **1/1325**. The available data about BC on the internet does not suggest that diabetes and BC are related. There is always the possibility that both are related to some common genetic factor.

17. The various expected values, EA, EB, EC, and ED are: EA = (1/10($2) = 20 cents; EB = (2/10)($2) = 40 cents; EC = (4/10)($2) = 80 cents; ED = (3/10)($2) = 60 cents. So **A is worst, C is best**.

19. The probability of a single number winning on a wheel is 1/38. So the **expected value on a payout** of $36 is (1/38)36 = **$ 0.95**. So the **expected value of the bet** is $0.95 - $1.00 = **-5 cents**.

21. To be a fair game the cost to play should equal the expected value. EV = (1/6)1 + (1/6)2 + (1/6)3 + (1/6)4 + (1/6)5 + (1/6) 6 = 3.5. So the cost to play should be **$3.50**.

23. If 3 lengths, say a, b, and c, are to be the sides of a triangle then the sum of any 2 of these sides must be greater than the third side. Now, assume that the first break is left of the middle of the stick, say at point x:

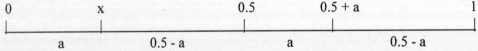

The second break must be at a point between 0.5 and (0.5 + a) because if it were between (0.5 + a) and 1 the middle piece would be greater than 0.5 and no triangle would be formed. On the other hand, if the first break is at a point greater than 0.5,

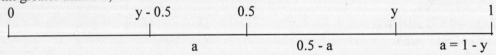

then the second break must be in the region y - 0.5 and 0.5 otherwise once again the middle piece would be greater than 0.5. So we can simulate this by drawing a pair of random numbers between 0 and 1 to represent the points of the first and second breaks. Based on the coordinate of the first break we can calculate the locations for the second break that would allow a triangle to be formed. For example, one such pair is (0.39, 0.14). Since 0.39 is less than 0.5, the possible triangle forming locations for break 2 are between 0.5 and 0.89. Since 0.14 is not in this range, no triangle will be formed. A second pair is (0.79, 0.33). Since 0.79 is greater than 0.5 the acceptable region for triangle formation is 0.29 to 0.5. Since 0.33 is in this region a triangle will be formed. A computer run of 100 such experiments resulted in 48 triangles formed. So the probability of a triangle being formed in 0.48.

25. The P(live to 75 given age 50) is 0.73, about 8/11, and P(not live to 75 given age 50) is about 1 - 8/11, 3/11. So the odds in favor of living to age 75 given age 50 are (8/11) / (3/11) = **8/3**.

SECTION 9.5

1. a. Because the number of children in a family is represented by a whole number, a **discrete** random variable is appropriate.
   b. Although the measurement of money is discrete, the increment, cents, is so small with respect to the totals involved, treating net worth as a **continuous** random variable is appropriate.
   c. The cholesterol level is measured on a scale of roughly 0 to 500 with increments of 1. Although the increments are discrete they are sufficiently small with respect to the total values to treat the cholesterol levels as a **continuous** random variable.
   d. The 3 sums showing after rolling two dice vary by one over a small range are best represented with a **discrete** random variable.

3. The possible outcomes for throwing a single die are 1 dot, 2 dots, 3 dots, up to six dots, each with a probability of 1/6. The probability distribution is discrete because the dots are represented by the first six counting numbers which form a discrete set. The graph is:

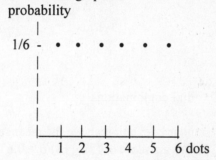

5. Assuming that the machine will make its cuts randomly with equal probabilities for any length, the probability that the longer piece will be less than 5 inches is **0.25**. Consider the representation of the piece of licorice:

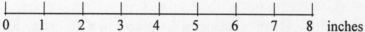

   If a cut is made to the left of 3 or to the right of 5, then the longer piece will be greater than 5 inches. So a cut must be made between the 3 and 5 inch marks to produce longer pieces less than 5 inches. P(3< cut <5) = 1/4.

7. Since $z = (x - u)/s$ where x is the raw score, u the mean score, s the standard deviation we have:
   a. $z = (56 - 50)/4 = $ **1.5**.
   b. $z = (19 - 31)/ 5.5 = $ **-2.18**.
   c. $z = (57 - 110) / 15 = $ **-3.53**.
   d. $z = (13 - 15) / 4.5 = $ **-0.44**.

9. The expected value, EV, for the number of persons living in a household is the same as the average number and is: $EV \geq (0.25)1 + (0.30)2 + (0.15)3 + (0.16)4 + (0.08)5 + (0.03)6 + (0.02)7 + (0.01)8$. So EV ≥ **2.74 or 3 persons**.

11. a. Because the area under the graph is a triangle with base 2 and altitude 1, the area, (1/2)base x altitude, = 1.
    b. The probability associated with the value 1.5 is 0.5.
        The probability of a sum less than 1.5 is the area under the graph up to the vertical through 1.5. This area is the total area, 1, minus the area of the triangle 0.5 by 0.5. So the probability is $1 - (1/2)(0.5)(0.5) = $ **0.875.**

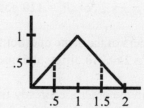

    c. The probability of a sum less that 0.5 is the area under the graph up to the vertical through 0.5. This area is $(1/2)(0.5)(0.5) = $ **0.125.**

13. The z value for a time of 73 sec is (73 - 85)/12 = 1 standard deviation below the mean. Table 9.2 shows that 34.13% of normally distributed values fall between the mean and one standard deviation below the mean. So 50% - 34.13 %, 15.87 %, values can be expected to be lower than 1 standard deviation below the mean. Thus the probability of a run less than 73 sec is **0.1587**.

15. a. Fifteen oz is [(15 - 16)/0.8], 1.25 standard deviations below the mean. The probability of a value being between 1.25 standard deviations below the mean and the mean is 0.3944. Thus the probability of a value being more than 1.25 standard deviations below the mean is 0.5000 - 0.3944 = **0.1056**.
  b. Seventeen and a half oz is 1.875 standard deviations above the mean. The probability of a value being between the mean and 1.875 standard deviations above the mean is about 0.47. So the probability of a value being above 17.5 oz is about **0.03**.

17. Each dial can show A, B, or C with the same probability, 1/3, Thus each of the 9 possible outcomes, AA, AB, AC, BA, BB, BC, CA, CB, CC are equally likely with a probability of 1/9.

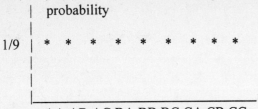

```
    |   probability
    |
1/9 |  *  *  *   *   *   *   *  *  *
    |
    |
    |_____
       AA AB AC BA BB BC CA CB CC    dial combinations
```

19. Cheryl has a z score of (600 - 500)/100 = 1 standard deviation above the mean, a score better than about 84 % of those taking the SAT. Becky, on the ACT, had a z score of (22 - 18)/6 = 0.67. Becky scored better than about 75% of those taking the ACT. Cheryl scored better relative to her peers than did Becky relative to her peers. If the tests are equivalent and if the populations taking the tests are equivalent, Cheryl performed better than Becky.

21. One hundred calls per minutes is (100 - 84)/16 = 1 standard deviation above the mean. Since 0.3413 of values can be expected to be between the mean and a z of 1 and another 0.5 of values can be expected to fall below the mean, the probability that there will be less than 100 call per minute is 0.8413. So the probability that there will be more than 100 calls per minute and the switchboard will be overloaded is about **15.87%**.

23. Responses will vary with the research of students

SECTION 9.6

1. a. If 0 is allowed in the first position then the are 5 possible numbers for the first digit, 5 for the second, 5 for the third, and five for the fourth. There are 5 x 5 x 5 x 5 = **625** possible combinations.
  b. Again assuming that 0 may be used in the first position but that repetitions are not allowed, we have 5 possibilities for the first digit, 4 for the second, 3 for the third, and 2 for the fourth.
   There are 5 x 4 x 3 x 2 , or $_5P_4$ = **120** possible plates.

2. Since different orders of the same questions are to be considered as different tests, there are $_{14}P_5$ different tests. $_{14}P_5$ = 14!/(14-5)! = **240,240** different 5 question tests.

3. Since 3 positions in the order are already fixed, then there are 6 possibilities for the 4th position, 5 for the 5th, 4 for the 6th, 3 for the 7th, 2 for the 8th, and the remaining player fills the last remaining position. So there are 6 x 5 x 4 x 3 x 2 x 1 = **720** possible batting orders with 3 positions fixed.

5. In order for each team to play every other team once, each of the eight teams must play 7 games. To play every other team twice, then, the total number of games is 8 x 7 x 2 = 112. But we are counting games such as AB twice, once as a game for A playing B and again as a game for B playing A. So the total number of distinct games is (1/2) if 112, **56**.

7. The coins may be selected individually, in pairs, in threes, in fours, and finally in 1 group of 5. The order of selection is not important and no grouping has the same value as any other grouping. So the total number of combinations is: $_5C_1 + {_5C_2} + {_5C_3} + {_5C_4} + {_5C_5} = 5 + 10 + 10 + 5 + 1 = \textbf{31}$.

9. Ignoring order, the number of ways of selecting 9 persons from a pool of 20 persons is $_{20}C_9$ which is 20!/(20-9)!9! = **167,960**.

11. Since order is not important we have: $_{52}C_5 = 52!/(52-5)!5! = \textbf{2,598,960}$ different 5 card hands.

13. Represent the license plate number D1 D2 D3 D4. D1 must come from the set {1,2,3,4,5}. Thus there are 5 possibilities for D1. Now, for each D1 there are 5 possibilities for D2 from the set {0,1,2,3,4,5}. There are 5 possibilities, not 6, because consecutive digits cannot repeat because license plates must be unique. D4 has 3 possibilities, the set {0,2,4}, because the license number must be even. So that leaves 4 possibilities for D3 from the set {0,1,2,3,4,5}. There are only 4 possibilities because D3 cannot repeat on the left or the right. The total is 5 x 5 x 4 x 3 = **300**. The same argument hold for odd numbers except that D4 must come from {1,3,5}. So there are also **300** different odd license plates.

15. Suppose the offices are P, V, S, and T. P can be filled in 6 ways, V in 5 ways, S in 4, and T in 3. So the total is 6 x 5 x 4 x 3 = **360, or** $_6\textbf{P}_4$.

17. Because order is not important the total number of different committees is $_{57}C_8 \times {_{43}C_4} = \textbf{2.039 x 10}^{14}$.

19. There are 6 possible colors to face up. For each of these 6 there are 4 colors to face forward.

Up	Forward
R	OYGB
V	OYGB
O	BRYV
G	BRYV
Y	ORGV
B	ORGV

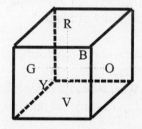

So there are **24** orientations.

21. $_nC_r = n!/[(n-r)!r!]$ and $_nC_{n-r} = n!/[n-(n-r)]!(n-r)! = n!/r!(n-r)!$. So $_nC_r = {_nC_{n-r}}$.

23. If seated in a line there are 5 possibilities for the first position, 4 for the second, 3 for the third, 2 for the fourth, and 1 for the last. Thus there are 5 x 4 x 3 x 2 x 1 = **120** different arrangements.

25. An estimated number of variations is (10)(30)(20)(10) = 60,000. The actual value is (12)(30)(18)(10) = 64,800.

27. Strategies for writing all combinations will vary. Now, the first number of the combination can be any of ten numbers, 0 through 9. For each of these, the second number can be any of 9 numbers because repetitions are not allowed. The remaining number can be any of the eight remaining numbers. So there are a total of 10 x 9 x 8, 720 combinations. At, say 6 trials per minute, it would take 120 minutes, about **2 hours** to test all combinations.

29.

n	n!	n^2
1	1	1
2	2	4
3	6	9
4	24	16
5	120	25
6	720	26

After n=3, n! grows at a faster rate than does the exponential n^2.
So 1/n! will decrease at a faster rather than will $1/n^2$.

CHAPTER 9 REVIEW EXERCISES

1. a. The sample space for tossing three coins is: {HHH,HHT,HTH,THH,TTH,THT,HTT,TTT}.
    b. The subset with T in the second position is {HTH,TTH,HTT,TTT}.
    c. The event H on the third toss is {HHH,HTH,THH,TTH}.
    d. The event of H on the second toss and T on the third toss is {HHT,THT}.

3. a. P(JD and E) = (1/52)(3/6) = **1/104**.
    b. P(R and n≥3) = (26/52)(4/6) = **1/3**.
    c. P(F and 5) = (16/52)(1/6) = **2/39**.

5. a. The uniform sample space for tossing 2 dice is {11,12,13,14,15,16,21,22,23,24,25,26,31,32,33,34,35,36,41, 42,43, 44,45,46,51,52,53,54,55,56,61,62,63,64,65,66}. Of these the sum 7 can be obtained in 6 ways, the sum 8 in 5 ways, the sum 9 in 4 ways, the sum 10 in 3 ways, the sum 11 in 2 ways ,and the sum 12 in 1 way. Thus the event space for a sum of 7 or greater has 21 elements and a probability of **21/36**.
    b. Two of the 36 elements of the sample space show one 3 and one five. So the probability is **2/36**.
    c. The first die can be 1, 3, or 5 and for each of these the second can be 1, 3, or 5. So there are 9 outcomes with both numbers odd. So the probability is **9/36**.
    d. Of the 36 outcomes, 9 are even/even, 9 are odd/odd, 9 are even/odd, and 9 are odd/even. So 27 outcomes have at least 1 die even. Additionally, there are 3 odd/odd combinations with a sum of 6. Thus the event has 30 of the 36 outcomes and a probability of **30/36**.

7. Since this situation deals with two draws without replacement, the sample space, as opposed to problem #2 in this section, will change after the first draw.
    a. The probability of 2 red marbles is **0** because if a red marble is drawn first it is not replaced. So the sample space for the second draw does not contain any red marbles. Thus the probability of a red on the second draw is 0.
    b. Since P(R on 1st) is 1/4 and P(G on 2nd given R on first) is 1/3, the probability of first drawing red and then drawing green is (1/4)(1/3) = **1/12**.. An alternative approach is to examine the 12 equally likely outcomes, for each possible 1st draw there are 3 equally likely second draws, a total of 12. One of these 12 is R-G.
    c. The sample space of 12 equally likely outcomes is R-B, R-G, R-Y, B-R, B-G, B-Y, G-R, G-B, G-Y, Y-R, Y-G, Y-B. Note that 2 of the 12 have at least one R and one G. Thus the probability is **2/12 = 1/6**.
    d. Six of the 12 equally likely outcomes have no yellow (Y). Thus the probability of no Y is **6/12 = 1/2**.

9. Expected value = sum of the (probability times outcome) products.
    So EV = 0.15(0) + 0.35(10 000) + 0.2(20 000) + 0.3(55 000). So the EV is **$9,000**.

11. a. Examination of the demographics shows that the populations of the states are far from equal. Comparisons of the populations suggest how likely it is for a person to live in a particular state. So one cannot consider a listing of the states to be a uniformly distributed sample space.

   b. These events are not mutually exclusive. The same person can attend both a 2-year and a 4-year institution of higher learning.

   c. Because missing a free throw and making a free throw are complementary events, the sum of the probabilities must be 1.

13. The teacher has 15 choices for seating a student at the first desk, 14 for the second desk, and so on down to 1 student at the last desk. So there are **15!** different arrangements possible: about **1.3 x 10^{12}**.

15. Mutually exclusive events are those that have no common outcomes in the two event spaces. As an example, the events of an even number on a roll of a die and an odd number on the same roll of the die are mutually exclusive. The events of rolling an even number and rolling a prime number are not mutually exclusive because one even number, 2, is also a prime. Independent events are events in which the outcome of one does not affect the outcome of the other. For example, if the same die is rolled twice the outcome of the second roll is not affect by the outcome of the first roll. The probability of obtaining, say, a six on the second roll is 1/6 no matter what happen on the first roll. The probability of the second roll producing an even sum obviously is dependent upon the outcome of the first roll of the die.

17. The prime factorization of 105 is 3 x 5 x 7. One of these numbers is the number of meats, another the number of toppings (onions, peppers, olives, etc.), and the third the number of cheeses. It is reasonable to assume 5 meats and 7 toppings. So that leaves **3** for the number of cheeses.

19. Assume that the kernel of corn falls either into one of the silos or into the inner area bounded by the silos. Each silo has an area of $(3.14)(20)^2$, 1256 sq ft. So the four together have an area 5024 sq ft. The square formed by joining the centers of the silos has an area of 40 ft x 40 ft = 1600 sq ft. Each of the shaded portions is one quarter of a silo circle and, all together, make up one circle with an area 1256 sq ft. So the event space, the area inside the small square but not in the silos has an area of 1600 - 1256 = 344 sq ft. Thus the probability of landing in this area is **344/(5024+344) ≈ 0.064** .

21. A tree diagram begins 3 blank branches. For each of these blank branches there are 5 position branches. For each of the position branches there are 3 branches, either do not remove metal at that position or remove it at one of two different depths. So there are (3)(5)(3), **45**, different keys.

23. The area of the bull's eye, the event space, is 4π. The area of the first dark ring is (36 - 16)π, the area of the second dark ring is (100 - 64)pi. So the entire shaded area, the sample space, has an area of (4 + 20 + 36)π. This the probability of a bull's eye given landing in the shaded area is 4π/60πi = **4/60 = 1/15**.

SECTION 10.1

1.   Responses will vary. Students may associate geometric patterns with groups of stars, circles and ellipses with planetary motions, various shapes with clouds. They may see various polygons and polyhedra in houses.

3.   The sides of a Golden rectangle are in the ratio 1.618..:1. Since 5:3 = 1.66..:1 and 8:5 = 1.6:1, the 5 x 8 card is closer to the dimensions of the Golden rectangle than is the 3 x 5 card.

5.   The selection made by students will vary. They may select book covers, building fronts, entrances to formal rooms, or the like. The ratio should be close to 1.618..:1.

7.
Polyhedron	F	V	F + V	E
Triangular prism	5	6	11	9
Pentagonal pyramid	6	6	12	10
Rectangular pyramid	5	5	10	8

Since F + V = E + 2, Euler's formula holds.

9.   Trial shows that nets **a and b** can be folded to form open-top boxes.

11. a.   Slicing the cone produces an ellipse.
     b.   Slicing the cylinder produces a rectangle.

13.

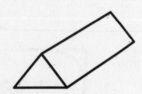

15. The ratios are: 1:1 = 1; 2:1 = 2; 3:2 = 1.5; 5:3 ≈ 1.66; 8:5 = 1.6; 13:8 = 1.625; 21:13 ≈ 1.615; 34:21 ≈ 1.619; 55:34 ≈ 1.6176; 89:55 ≈ 1.618; 144:89 ≈ 1.617977; 233:144 ≈ 1.61805; 377:233 ≈ 1.61802575; 610:377 ≈ 1.61803713. The golden ratio is 1.618033989...

17. The first sixteen terms of the Fibonacci sequence are:1,1,2,3,5,8,13,21,34,55,89,144,233,377,610,987. It appears that the even terms are bracketed by pairs of odd terms. So the even terms appear to be those terms in the sequence with location numbers that are multiples of 3. So about 1/3 of Fibonacci numbers are even. Of the first 25 numbers, 8 will be even. Extending the Fibonacci sequence started above through the first 25 numbers: 1,597, 2,584, 4,181, 6,765, 10,946, 17,711, 28,657, 46,368, 75,025 and counting the even numbers shows the relation to hold.

19. The reciprocal of the Golden Ratio is 1/1.618034.. ≈ 0.618033 and 1.618034 - 1 = 0.618033. These are the numbers found in exercise 18, numbers such that their difference and their product both equal 1.

21. a. For the square antiprism F = 10, V = 8, E = 16, and F + V = 18. Since F + V = E + 2, Euler's theorem holds.

   b. For the triangular antiprism, we may first envision 2 triangles, ABC and DEF in parallel planes. Each vertex of the top triangle, ABC, is joined to 2 points of the lower triangle producing 3 faces and each vertex of the lower triangle is joined to 2 points of the upper triangle producing 3 more faces. Combined with the upper and lower triangles as faces we have we have F = 8, V = 6, and E = 12. Since F + V = E + 2, Euler's Theorem holds.

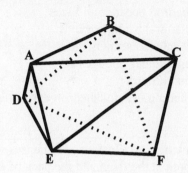

23.

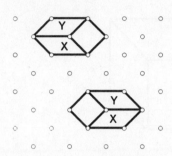

25. The figure formed, as shown, is a hexagon. If a Coordinate system is superimposed on the cube with side s, the vertices of the hexagon KLMNPQ are (0,s,s/2), (s/2,s,s), (0,s/2,0), (s,s/2,s), (s/2,0,0), and (s,0,s/2) respectively. Each of the sides of the hexagon is the hypotenuse of an isosceles triangle with legs of length s/2 and has a length of $(s/2)\sqrt{2}$. Now, if the triangles MKL, KLN, LNQ, NQP, QPM, and PMK are congruent then the interior angles are congruent and the hexagon is regular. Applying the distance formula to the third side of each of the 6 triangles [for example: triangle MKL. ML =

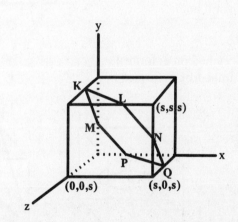

$\sqrt{[(0-s/2)^2+(s/2-s)^2+(0-s)^2]} = s\sqrt{(3/2)}]$ we find that the lengths are all $s\sqrt{(3/2)}$. So the triangles are congruent and the figure is a **regular hexagon**.

27. a. In order to fit about an edge with no gaps or overlaps the sum of the dihedral angles of the polyhedra must be 360°. The cube, with a dihedral angle of 90°, is the only polyhedron with a dihedral angle that is a factor of 360 and thus the only polyhedron that will fill the space about an edge.

   b. A combination of 2 tetrahedra and 2 octahedra, angle sum 2(70°32') + 2 (109°28') = 360°, will fill the space about an edge.

29. a.   The regular polyhedra that are deltahedra are **tetrahedra, octahedra, and icosohedra**.

b.   The double triangular pyramid is
a deltahedron because all faces
are equilateral triangles but it
is not regular as seen by the
different number of edges at
different vertices.
A tetrahedron is a deltahedron that **is** regular.

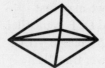

31. No, the drawings are illusions. Responses will vary. They may include statements as: A vertical support
cannot be both at the front and the back of a structure; or, by continually going down steps I cannot return to
my starting position.

33. Responses will vary. A possibility: A cube has
8 vertices, 12 edges, and 6 faces. So, for a cube,
edges + 2 = faces + vertices. Now, cutting off a
corner replaces 1 vertex with 3, and adds a face.
So the sum of the faces and vertices increases
by 3. But the cut produces three additional edges
for the added triangular face. So the difference
between F + V and E is still 2 and Euler's
Theorem still holds.

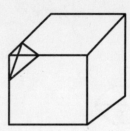

35. b.   An octahedron is formed
c.   A tetrahedron is formed

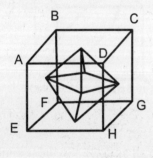

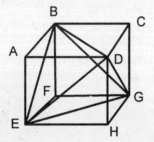

b.

c.

37. Using the Pythagorean theorem, we have:
$r^2 = 1^2 + (1/2)^2 = 1 + 1/4 = 5/4$. Thus
$r = (\sqrt{5})/2$. So CD = $1/2 + (\sqrt{5})/2 = (1 + \sqrt{5})/2$
and l/w = CD/AD = $[(1 + \sqrt{5})/2]$ /1, the Golden ratio.

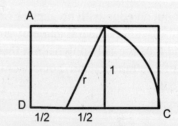

SECTION 10.2

1. The physical objects may call to mind:
    a. A line segment;
    b. Parallel lines;
    c. A ray or a bundle of rays;
    d. An angle;
    e. A regular octagon.

3.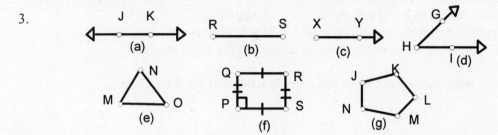

5. **Yes**. Two of the vertices, A and B, are odd. So one may begin at A or B and end at B or A respectively.

7. Responses will vary. Possibilities include:

    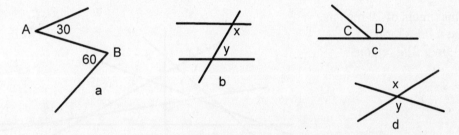

9. Responses will vary. They may include: Both squares and rhombi have all 4 sides congruent but squares are also rectangles and must have right angles. Every square *is* a rhombus but not every rhombus is a square. Kites must have 2 pairs of consecutive sides congruent. Since rhombi have all 4 sides congruents they have 2 pairs of consecutive sides congruent and thus all rhombi (and therefore squares) are kites but not all kites are rhombi.

11. Student activity. Responses will vary among students.

13. a. Because the propeller will superimpose upon itself when rotated 120° or a multiple of 120° about its center, it has rotational symmetry in multiples of 120° about the center.
     b. Because of the top and bottom stripes, the *flag* has two lines of reflection symmetry, a horizontal and a vertical through the middle of the star. The star itself has rotational symmetry in multiples of 60° and 6 lines of reflection symmetry, the lines through point angle vertices and the center and dent angle vertices and the center.
     c. A half turn will superpose the figure upon itself so it had rotational symmetry in multiples of 180° about its center.

15. The square prism has 3 planes,
a, b, and c of reflection symmetry
and 3 axes, x, y, and z of
rotation symmetry with angles of 90°.

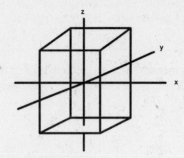
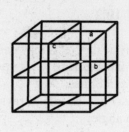

17. The processes will depend upon the GES used. In general,
    a. Congruent figures may be obtained by using a form of COPY command.
    b. The COPY command applies to all types of figures, angles as well as segments.
    c. Most GES has a BISECT command which will determine midpoints and angle bisectors.
    d. Same as c.
    e. Once a line and point have been drawn, GES has a construct PERPENDICULAR command.
    f. Same as e.

19. a. Not possible
       for 4 lines to
       intersect in exactly
       2 points.

       b.   c.   d.   e.

21. Six lines form a maximum of 10 regions.
You may note that n lines form a
maximum of $(n^2 - 3n + 2)/2$ regions.

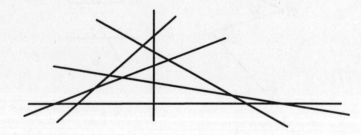

23. Responses will vary.

25. a. A kite that is not a rhombus has reflection symmetry over its long diagonal.
    b. A parallelogram that is not a rectangle has 180° rotational symmetry about its center.
    c. A rectangle has both rotational symmetry (180° about its center) and reflection symmetry (with respect to lines through the center perpendicular to the sides).

27. For the array there are 8 lines containing 3 points: 1-2-3, 4-5-6, 7-8-9, 1-4-7, 2-5-8, 3-6-9,
    1-5-9, and 3-5-7.   There are 12 lines containing 2 points: 1-8, 1-6, 2-4, 2-7,- 2-9, 2-6, 3-4,
    3-8, 4-9, 4-8, 6-7, 6-8. Thus there is a total of **20 lines**.

1	2	3
4	5	6
7	8	9

29. a. Assuming that the distance between adjacent horizontal and vertical pegs is one unit, the area of the smallest square is 1 sq unit.
    b. The area of the largest square that can be formed is 16 sq units.
    c. Other squares that can be formed have areas of **2, 4, 5, 8, 9, and 10 sq units** (figures below).
    d. **A square of area 6 cannot be constructed**. The side of such a square would be $\sqrt{6}$. To get this length on the Geoboard, if the lower left corner of the Geoboard is assigned coordinates (0,0) then there must be a peg with coordinates (x,y) such that $x^2 + y^2 = 6$, x and y integers. If x is 1, then $y = \sqrt{5}$; if x = 2, then $y = \sqrt{2}$. Thus there are no such x, y.
    Figures:

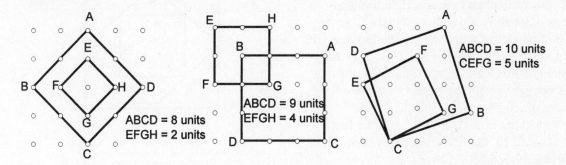

31. a. **Never**. The sum of the angles about a point is 360°. Two intersecting lines form 4 angles. If there are congruent, then each must be 90°, a right angle.
    b. **Always**. By definition, the angles formed upon bisection are congruent.
    c. **Always**. The exterior sides of linear angles form a straight angle. If the sum of 2 angles is a straight angles, then the angles are supplementary.
    d. **Always**. Vertical angles are formed by intersecting lines which form four pairs of linear angles. Linear angles are supplementary.
    e. **Sometimes**. Linear angles are supplementary angles with a common vertex. But any pair of angles with a sum of 180° are supplementary, part of the same figure or completely distinct.
    f. **Sometimes**. If the legs of a right triangle are congruent, then the right triangle is isosceles.
    g. **Sometimes**. If the rhombus has a right angle, then it is a square.
    h. **Always**. Since all 3 angles of an equilateral triangle measure 60°, the triangle is acute.
    i. **Never**. If a kite had a pair of parallel sides as does a trapezoid, then the kite would have 2 pairs of parallel sides making it a parallelogram. But a no trapezoid is a parallelogram.
    j. **Never**. A right triangle contains a right angle. The sum of the remaining 2 angles is 90° thus neither can be greater than 90° So the triangle has no angle greater than 90° and is not obtuse.
    k. **Sometimes**. A parallelogram that is both a rectangle and a rhombus is a square. But not all parallelograms are squares.
    l. **Always**. Since an equilateral triangle has all 3 sides congruent it necessarily has 2 sides congruent. An isosceles triangle is not restricted to 2 and only 2 congruent sides.
    m. **Never**. Because a parallelogram has 1 and only 1 pair of parallel sides, no parallelogram is a trapezoid.

33. A network is traversable is all vertices are of even degree or if 2 and only 2 are of odd degree.
   a. All vertices of a tetrahedron are of degree 3. Thus it is **not** traversable.
   b. All vertices of a cube are of degree 3. Thus it is **not** traversable
   c. All vertices of an octahedron are of degree 4. This it **is** traversable
   d. All vertices of a dodecahedron are of degree 3. This it is **not** traversable
   e. All vertices of a icosahedron are of degree 5. This it is **not** traversable

35. Suppose a side of the largest square is AB.
   Then a side of the first nested square, CD,
   is the hypotenuse of an isosceles right triangle
   with legs AB/2 and has length $(1/2)AB\sqrt{2}$.
   Similarly, the side of the second nested square, EF,
   is $(1/2)CD\sqrt{2} = 1/2[1/2(AB)\sqrt{2}]\sqrt{2} = (\sqrt{2}/2)^2 AB$.
   Continuing in this manner, and numbering the
   squares beginning with the largest as number 1,
   with sides of length s, a side of square n is
   $(\sqrt{2}/2)^{n-1}s$ and has area $(1/2)^{n-1}s^2$. So, If the first
   square has side 10, the first six squares have areas
   100, 50, 25, 12.5, 6.25, 3.125.

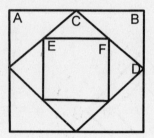

37. Responses will vary. Possibilities include: One could use the recovered piece to make duplicate pieces to be placed together, in whole or in part, to form a circle. Then the diameter could be measured. Another approach: trace the recovered arc of the circular wheel. Construct 2 chords and then the perpendicular bisectors of these chords. The bisectors intersect at the center of the circle of which the arc is a part. The radius could then be measured.

39.

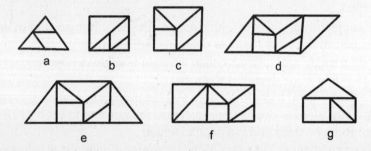

41   a   Responses will vary. One approach would be to take the cut-out triangles and use the smallest as the unit of area.   The areas of the other triangles could be estimated in terms of this unit.
   b. The triangles could be overlayed with the grid and the number of squares within each triangles estimated. Full squares inside the triangles are, of course, counted. Squares half or more in are counted; squares considered to be more than half out are not counted.

43.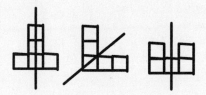

45.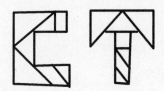

SECTION 10.3

1. If a regular polygon is to tessellate the plane its interior angles measure must be a factor of 360. The 108° interior angle measure of a regular pentagon is not a factor of 360.

3. Let the given triangle, ABC, be half of a parallelogram ABCD. Since all parallelograms tessellate, ABCD tessellates and hence ABC tessellates.

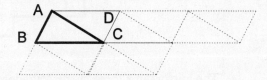

5. There are eight semi-regular tessellations.

7. Although the tessellation is accomplished with regular polygons, squares and equilateral triangles, the arrangements at all vertices are not identical, Thus the tessellation is not semi-regular.

9. Responses will vary. Regular polygons with interior angles with measures in degrees not factors of 360 will not tessellate. For example, an octagon has interior angles of 135° and will not tesselate.

11. A regular octagon will not tessellate a plane by itself because one cannot fit octagons about a point with no overlap or gaps. The interior angles of regular octagons are 135° and 135 is not a factor of 360. **Octagons and squares** will tessellate as shown.

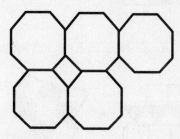

13.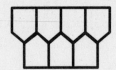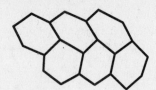

15. The vertex tessellation of the tessellation of regular hexagons is a semi-regular tessellation, 3,6,3,6 of equilateral triangles and regular hexagons.

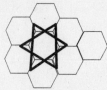

17. Responses will vary. One possibility is:
RIGHT 30: REPEAT 2[FD 30 RT 120]: FD 30:
RIGHT 30: REPEAT 2[FD 30 RT 90]:
FD 30

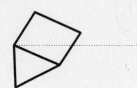

19. Two hexomino tessellations are:

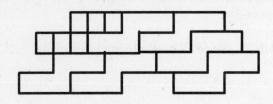 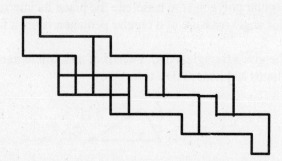

21.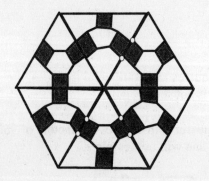

The mirrors in a three mirror kaleidoscope are at angles of 60 degrees. Thus each point of the pattern will be a vertex of three regular hexagons. Because of the symmetry of the pattern and the mirrors, the three regular hexagons will overlap and produce the hexagonal figure sketched at the left.

23. Two possible tessellations using squares and equilateral triangles are shown below.

25. Description will vary. The tessellation is formed from regular pentagons and regular decagons, 5-pointed stars, and figures made of 2 8-sided portions of decagons fitted together to form a 16-sided concave polygon.

27. Responses will vary.

29. Responses will vary. The drawing appears to begin with a pattern of quadrilaterals representing fields which smoothly become curved-sided figures which ultimately become representations of birds in the air.

SECTION 10.4

1. a. To identify a slide one needs to know both the direction and the magnitude of the slide of one point on the figure.
    b. To identify a turn one needs to know both the center of the rotation and the directed angle through which a segment joining the center to any point of the figure is rotated.
    c. To identify a flip or a reflection one needs to know only the line over which the reflection takes place.

3.

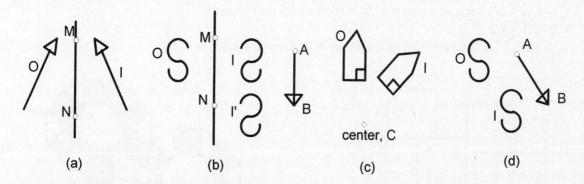

(a)   (b)   (c)   (d)

    a. A reflection over MN produces I, the image of O.
    b. In order to produce the desired image we may first reflect the object over MN and then translate this image with the vector AB.
    c. To produce the desired image we can rotate the object about centerC at an angle of -45°.
    d. To produce the desired image we can translate the object with the vector AB.

5. a. The pair is topologically equivalent because the W can be transformed into the spiral without any cutting. Just stretch the W into a segment and then form the spiral.
    b. The two figures are not topologically equivalent. The curved figure has a vertex of degree 4 that cannot be reduced by smoothing. The segmented figure has no vertex of degree 4. If the curved figure is cut at the 'leaves' to separate the 'stem and the roots', then a figure topologically equivalent to the segmented figure is produced.

7. The following sets contain topologically equivalent letter of the alphabet because the elements of a set may be transformed one into another without cutting:{A,R}, {C,I,LM,N,S,U,V,W,Z}, {E,F,G,Y,T}, {H,I}, {K,X}, {O,D}, {P,Q}. For example, all the elements of the second set can be 'straightened out' into segments and then reformed into any of the other elements.

9. a.

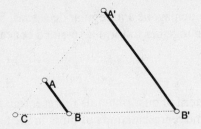

b. CA'/CA= **3/1** because the transformation $S_{C,3}$ was applied.
c. CB'/CB = **3/1** by the same reasoning as in b.
d. A'B'/AB = **3/1** because A'B' is the image of AB under a size transformation with a scale factor of 3.
e.

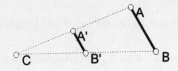

f. CA'/CA = **1/2** because a size transformation of 0.5 was applied.
g. CB'/CB = **1/2**
h. A'B'/AB = **1/2** because A'B' is the image of AB under a dilation of 1/2.

11.

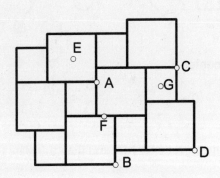

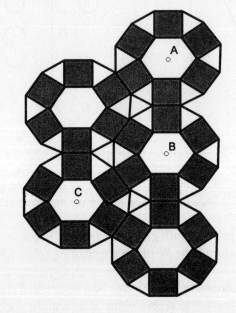

The first pattern can be translated from A to B, B to C, and A to C to be coincident with itself. It may also be rotated 180° about points located such as E, F, and G. There are no line of reflection.

The second pattern can be translated from the center of any hexagon, for example A, to any center, such as B or C. It may be rotated 180° about the center of any square, 120° about the center of any triangle, or 60° about the center of hexagon. It may be reflected over lines through the midpoints of opposite sides of the hexagons or over lines through opposite vertices of the hexagons.

13. Responses will vary.

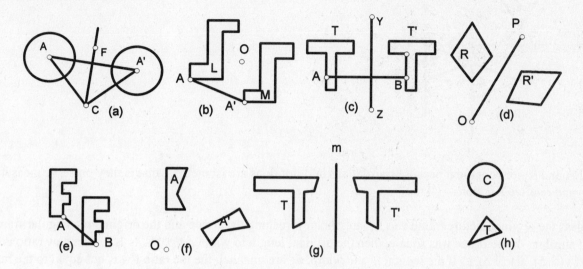

a. A --> A' by $T_{AA'}$, M_{CF}, or $R_{O,180}$.   b. L --> M by $T_{AA'}$, or $R_{O,180}$.   c. T --> T' by T_{AB} or M_{YZ}.
d. R --> R' by M_{OP} or $R_{O,60}$.   e. A --> B by T_{AB}.   f. A --> A' by $R_{O,60}$.
g. T --> T' by Mm

15.

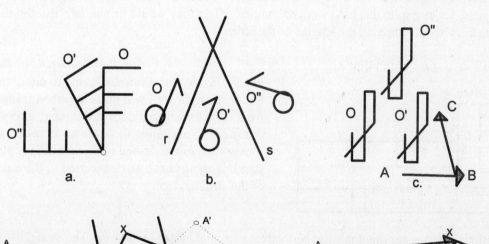

17.

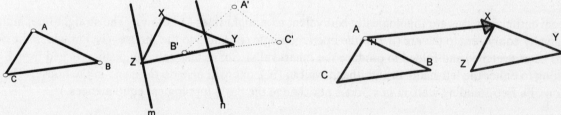

Gina
could have used 2 reflections: first a reflection of ABC over m producing A'B'C' and then a reflection of A'B'C' over n producing XYZ. The same effect could be produced by translating Abc by the vector AX.

19. a.

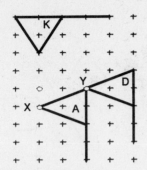

b. A and K are congruent because translations and rotations are isometries, that is they preserve measures and relative locations.

21. Unless the original picture frame was square, the new rectangular frame and the original rectangular frame are **not similar**. If the frame was square, then the original length to width ratio, s/s, is 1/1. The new ratio is (s+5)/(s+5), also 1 to 1. If the length, l, and width, w, are unequal, the the ratio l/w is not equal to the ratio (L+5)/(w+5). Consider as an example l = 10, w = 5. Then l/w = 2/1. Now the new dimensions are 15 and 10. The new ratio is 15/10 = 3/2. Since the ratios of corresponding dimensions are not equal, the figures are not similar.

23. There is no reason to expect the lots to be the same shape. Quadrilaterals, unlike triangles, are not rigid figures. Suppose, for example, that both were rectangles. Then they would be similar. But the shape of either could be changed without changing the lengths of the sides.

25. Responses will vary. One possibility is:

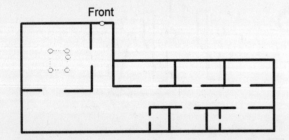

For the house plan shown, sticking to either the left or the right wall will guide a person from the front door to the front door and through every room of the house *providing* there are no 'free-standing' rooms such as the dashed room in the floor plan. Free-standing rooms have no connection to the outer walls of the structure.

Most conventional houses are topologically equivalent to straight lines (i. below). The straight line, in turn, is topologically equivalent to the arc (ii.), to the open rectangle (iii.), and to the 'house' (iv.) in which the outer wall has been stretched and folded to produce the inner walls. So: as one will obviously proceed from F to F by sticking to either the left-hand or right-hand wall in (ii.), one will also do the same in the house. The inclusion of a free-standing wall, m in v., does not change the basic topological equivalences.

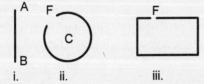

i. ii. iii. iv. v.

27. The answers are : **a. Yes;   b. No;   c. No;   d. Yes.** Supports for these conjecture will vary. Possibilities include:

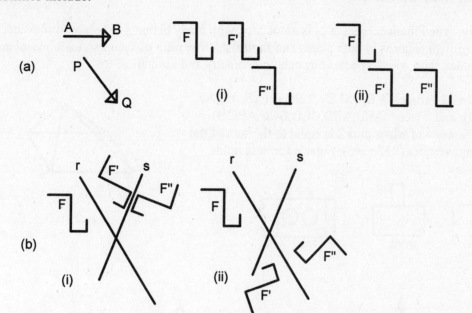

a. (A i and a ii above) are an example for which $T_{AB} * T_{PQ} = T_{PQ} * T_{AB}$.

b. The figures (b i and b ii above) show that reversing the order of reflections can results in different final images. Thus reflection is not commutative. In i reflection was first over then over s. Reflections in ii were in the opposite order.

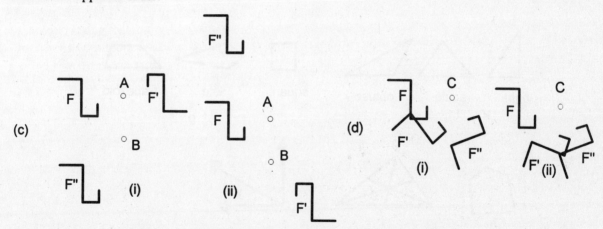

c. The figures (c i and cii above) above show that consecutive 180° rotations about different points do not produce coincident images.

d. The figures (d i and d ii above) support the conjecture that rotation about the same point is commutative.

CHAPTER 10 REVIEW EXERCISES

1.   Responses will vary. The Fibonacci sequence is associated with many patterns in nature. Fibonacci numbers describe the spiral growth patterns in both plants and shell fish. The ratio of successive Fibonacci numbers collapses to the Golden ratio which appears throughout geometry and aesthetics.

3.   A square pyramid has 5 vertices(A,B,C,D,E); 8 edges (AB,AD,AE, BE,ED,EC,BC,CD); and 5 faces (AEB,AED,CED,BCE,ABCD) 5 faces. Since the number of edges plus 2 is equal to the sum of the numbers of faces and vertices (8+2=5+5), Euler's formula holds.

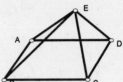

5.

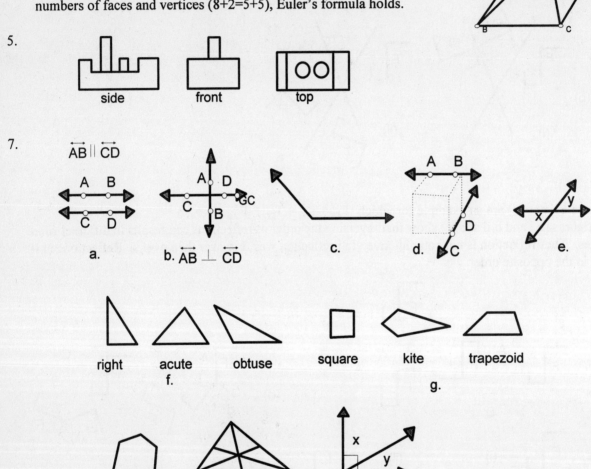

9. Vertices P and Q have odd degree. The other 3 vertices have even degree. So there is a path from P to Q. One such path is PCAQBPABCQ.

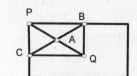

11. A right circular cone has an axis of symmetry through the center of its bases (AB) and an infinite number of axes which are perpendicular to the midpoint of the axis through the center such as CD and EF. The cylinder has a plane of symmetry (a) containing CD and EF and an infinite number of planes, such as b and,c containing AB.

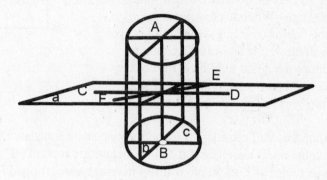

13 a. The tessellation is semi-regular because the arrangement of polygons a round all vertices is the same (8,8,4).

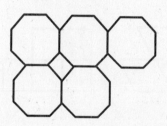

  b. A tessellation that uses regular polygons but with different arrangements at vertices is not semi-regular (for example figure 10.27 b).

15. a. There are an infinite number of possibilities. Two of these are:

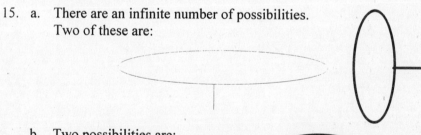

  b. Two possibilities are:

17. Although responses may vary, because 4, not 5, vertices are identified, there are 4 segments identifiable as sides. Thus it is a non-simple quadrilateral.

19. Responses will vary. Both congruence and size relations preserve the identity of the figures, that is both preserve shape: the relative lengths of segments and the sizes of angles. Congruence relations also preserve the absolute lengths of segments but size transformations preserve only the relative lengths.

21. Jared can use the properties of similar triangles. For example, suppose AB represents the tree and EF represents Jared between his eyes, F, and his feet, E. AC is the shadow of the tree. Jared begins outside the shadow and walks toward the tree. When his feet enter the shadow he begins counting steps until his eyes enter the shadow. He records the count, n. He continues the count until he is next to the tree and records the total, t, number of steps. By similarity, AB/EF = t/n, so AB = EF(t/n).

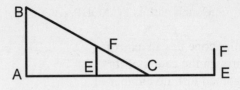

23. a. The rhombus will tessellate if it and its images are translated (slid) according to the vectors AB and AC.
     b. The square will tessellate if it and its images are rotated 90° about the corners.
     c. The rectangle will tessellate if it and its images are flipped (reflected) about its sides.

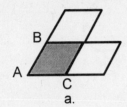 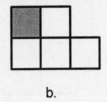 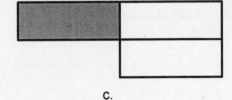

a.   b.   c.

SECTION 11.1

1. a. Alternate interiors: angles d and f, angles c and e.
    b. Corresponding angles: pairs: a and e; d and g; b and f; c and h.
    c. Alternate exterior angles: pairs a and h, b and g.
    d. Same side interiors: angles d and e, angles c and f.
    e. Congruent angles: answers will vary. Possibilities include: opposite exterior angles b and g; corresponding angles a and e; alternate interior angles d and f.
    f. Supplementary angles: answers will vary. Possibilities include: same side interiors d and e; same side exterior angles a and g.

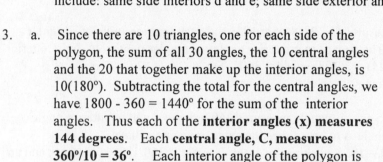

3. a.   Since there are 10 triangles, one for each side of the polygon, the sum of all 30 angles, the 10 central angles and the 20 that together make up the interior angles, is 10(180°). Subtracting the total for the central angles, we have 1800 - 360 = 1440° for the sum of the interior angles.   Thus each of the **interior angles (x) measures 144 degrees.**   Each **central angle, C, measures 360°/10 = 36°**.   Each interior angle of the polygon is supplementary to an exterior angle (y). So each **exterior angle measures 180 - 144 = 36°.**

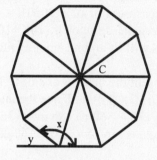

    b. Applying the same reasoning to a 12-sided polygon, **an interior angles measures [12(180) - 360)]/12 = 150°, a central angle measures 360/12 = 30°, an exterior angle 30°**.
    c. Applying the same reasoning to a 9-sided polygon, **an interior angles measures [9(180) - 360)]/9 = 140°, a central angle measures 360/9 = 40°,, an exterior angle 40°.**

5. Since home plate is a pentagon, the sum of the interior angles is (5-2)180 = 540°. Three of the angles of the plate are right angles, so the sum of the remaining 2 angles is 540 - 3(90) = 270°. Since they are congruent, each is 270/2 = **135°**.

7. The sum of the each of the 100 interior-exterior angle pairs at each vertex is 180°. So the sum of all the interior and exterior angles is 18,000°. The sum of the exterior angles of any convex polygon is 360°. So the sum of the interior angles of the 100-gon is 18,000° - 360° = **17,640°**·

9. The sum of the measures of the angles of a triangle is 180°. So <C + 37 + 59 = 180 and <C = **84°**.

11. Responses will vary. Possibilities include:
    a. <1 is congruent to <5 because they are corresponding angles formed by 2 parallels and a transversal. Angles 5 and 7 are supplementary because they are a linear pair. Thus m<5 +m<7 = 180 and substituting <1 for <5, m<1 + m<7 = 180. Since the sum of these 2 angles is 180, by definition they are supplementary angles.

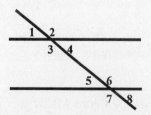

    b. Angles 5 and 1 are congruent because they are corresponding angles formed by 2 parallels and a transversal. But vertical angles 5 and 8 are congruent. We have <5 ≅ <1 and <5 ≅<8. So <1 ≅ <8 because they are congruent to the same angle.

13. Suppose angles x and y are the acute angles of a right triangle with z the right angle. Then
     m<x + m<y + m<z = 180° and m<x + m<y + 90° =180° and m<x + m<y = 90° degrees. But if the sum of 2
     angles is 90⁰, then those 2 angles are complementary. Thus the acute angles of a right triangle are
     complementary.

15. The sum of the measures of angles 1, 2, and 10 and also of angles 5, 6, and 7 is 180 degrees because they are
     sets of interior angles of triangles. The sum the measures of angles 3, 4, 8, and 9 is 360 degrees because they
     are a set of interior angles of a quadrilateral. Thus the sum of the measures of
     angles 1 through 10 is 720 degrees. This sum can be written as
     m<1 + (m<2 + m<3) + (m<4 + m<5) + m<6 + (m<7 + m<8) + (m<9 + m<10) = 720°. Written this way, the
     sum, 720°, of the 6 terms is the sum of the interior angles of the hexagon.

17. Each interior angle of a regular pentagon measures (5 - 2)180/5 = 108° and each interior angle of a regular
     decagon measures (10 - 2)(180)/10 = 144°. The sum of two interior angles of regular pentagons and 1 interior
     angle of a regular decagon is (108 +108 + 144) = 2(108) + 144 = 360°. So
     the figures will fit around a point with no gaps or overlaps.

19. Let n represent the number of sides. Then an exterior angle measures 360/n degrees and an interior angle
     measures (n - 2)(180)/n. Since the interior angle is to be 8 times the exterior angle we have
     8(360/n) = 180 - (360/n). So n = 9(360)/180 = **18**. Checking, an exterior angle is 360/18 = 20 degrees and an
     interior angle is (16/18)(180) = 160 degrees. And 160 is 8 times 20.

21. If each interior angle of a regular polgon is 157.5 degrees, then, because interior and exterior angles are
     supplementary, each exterior angle is 22.5 degrees. The sum of the exterior angles of a convex polygon is 360
     degrees. Because each of the exterior angles of this polygon is 22.5 degrees, there are 360/22.5 = **16 sides**.

23. The figure EFGH appears to
     be a **square**. If constructed with
     GES we find EH ≅ FG and
     EF ≅ HG and that angles
     E, F, G, and H are right angles.

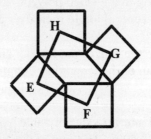

25. GES gives:

<ABC	<BCD	<BCD	<BDC + < BCD
95	50	45	95
150	90	60	150
155	115	40	155
55	30	25	55

     It appears that the measure of an exterior angle of a triangle is equal to the sum of the measures of the two
     non-adjacent interior angles.

27. GES shows the figure ABCD is
     a parallelogram.

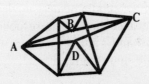

29. a. For 5 points there are 16 regions.

b.

points	regions
2	2
3	4
4	8
5	16

The pattern appears to be that if n is the number of points then the number of regions is 2^{n-1}. Using this conjecture to predict the number of regions for 6 points, we predict $2^5 = 32$ regions.

c. The figures shows that there are actually 31 regions, not 32. So, 6 points produce only 31 regions.

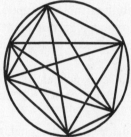

31. To fit around a point without gaps or overlaps, the sum of the 3 interior angles of the 3 polygons must equal 360 degrees.

polygon	triangle	quad	pentagon	hexagon	heptagon	octagon	nonagon	decagon	dodecagon	20-gon
int angle	60	90	108	120	(5/7)180	135	140	144	150	162

polygon	15-gon	18-gon	24-gon	42-gon
int angle	156	160	165	(20/21)180

If the polygons are identical, then each angle must be 360/3 = 120. So the only set of 3 identical polygons are 3 **hexagons. Two pentagons and a decagon** will work because 360 - 2(108) = 144. If one is a square then the sum of the angles of the other 2 must add to 360 - 90 = 270. So we have **a square and 2 octagons, a square + a pentagon + a 20-gon, and a square + a hexagon + a 12-gon.** Combinations that include an : equilateral triangle are: **triangle + 7-gon + 42-gon; triangle + 8-gon + 24-gon; triangle + 9-gon + 18-gon; triangle + 10-gon + 15-gon; triangle + 12-gon + 12-gon.**

33. The method is correct. The sum of the interior angles of a regular polygon is (n - 2)(180) degrees, n representing the number of sides. So each interior angle is (n - 2)(180)/n which is equal to 180 - 360/n. But the sum of the n central angles is 360. So each central angle has a measure of 360/n. Thus each of the interior angles has a measure equal to 180 minus the measure of a central angle.

35. Responses depend on group activity. Possible responses include: For an angle of 120 degrees an equilateral triangle is seen; for 90 degrees, a square; for 72 degrees, a regular pentagon. When the m<x is a factor of 360°, a regular polygon of 360/m<x sides can be seen.

37. For each of the n sides there is a triangle with an angle sum of 180 degrees. So the sum of all the angles is 180 n. Subtracting the sum of all the angles at the point inside the polygon, 360 degrees, we are left with 180 n - 360 = 180 n - 2(180) = (n - 2)180. This sum is the sum of all the remaining angles of the n triangles which make up the interior angles of the polygon.

SECTION 11.2

1.   Responses will vary. Possibilities include:
   a.   Centroid: geometrically, the centroid is the point of intersection of the medians. Physically, the centroid the center of mass or the point of balance.
   b.   Circumcenter: the circumcenter is the center of that circle that circumscribes a triangle, that circle for which the sides of the triangle are chords. The circumcenter is at the intersection of the perpendicular bisectors of the sides of the triangle.
   c.   The orthocenter is located at the intersection of the altitudes of a triangle.
   d.   The incenter is the center of that circle inscribed within the triangle, the circle tangent to the three sides of the triangle. The incenter is located at the intersection of the angle bisectors.

3.   Responses will vary. Possibilities include: suppose a, b, and c are the sides of a right triangle with c the side opposite the right angle. From an algebraic point of view:. Then $c^2 = a^2 + b^2$. From a geometric point of view, the area of the square with side c is equal to the sum of the areas of the squares with sides a and b.

5.   The diagonal of a square is also the longest side of a right triangle with legs equal in length to the sides of the square. So $d^2 = 120^2 + 120^2$. Therefore $d = 120\sqrt{2} \approx 120(1.414) \approx 169.7$ ft.

7.   Applying the Pythagorean theorem the diagonal, d, is: $d = \sqrt{[15.5^2 + 19.5^2]} = 24.91$ or **25 inches**.

9.   Using the Pythagorean theorem we have the height, h, is $\sqrt{[6^2 - 2^2]} = 4\sqrt{2} \approx$ **5.66 feet**.

11.   The diagonal of the doorway is $\sqrt{(6.5^2 + 3^2)} \cong 7.16$ ft.
   So the 7 ft square piece of plywood **can be carried** through the doorway.

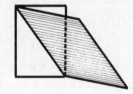

13.   The diagonals should be $\sqrt{(84^2 + 48^2)} = 12\sqrt{(65)} \approx$ **96.75 ft**.

15.   Each line is the hypotenuse of a right triangle with legs 5 ft and 12 ft. So the hypotenuse is 13 ft. Since 3 lines are required, the length of rope required for the three lines is **39 feet**.

17.   **a, b, d, e, g, and i** ensure that a quadrilateral is a parallelogram. c, h, and j could also describe an trapezoid and f is true for a kite.

19.   Yes, every generalization about a parallelogram, a rectangle, and a rhombus also hold for a square. Every square is a member of the sets parallelograms, rectangles, and rhombi although the converse is not the case: that is all rectangles, parallelograms, and rhombi are not squares.

21.   s is the hypotenuse of a right triangle with legs 4" and 10". So $s = \sqrt{(4^2 + 10^2)} = 2\sqrt{29} \approx$ **10.77"**.

23.   For three numbers a, b, and c, c the largest, if $a^2 + b^2 = c^2$ then the numbers can represent the sides of a right triangle. So:
   a. $(\sqrt{3})^2 + (\sqrt{4})^2 = (\sqrt{7})^2$: **yes**.   b. . $3^2 + 0.4^2 = 0.5^2$: **yes**.   c. $24^2 + 10^2 = 26^2$: **yes**.   d. $3^2 + 2^2 < 4^2$: **no**.

25.

s	$d = \sqrt{(s^2 + s^2)}$
2	2.828
3	4.143
4	5.657
5	7.07

The length of the diagonal is 1.414 times the length of a side.
The factor 1.4141 is an approximation of $\sqrt{2}$.
The diagonal of a square is the hypotenuse of a right triangle in which
  both legs are sides of the square. so:
$\sqrt{(s^2 + s^2)} = \sqrt{(2s^2)} = s\sqrt{2} = d \cong 1.414s$.

27. GES software suggests that the segment joining the
     midpoints of the nonparallel sides of a trapezoid is
     equal to one half of the sum of the lengths of the
     bases.

m $\overline{AB}$ = 0.44 inches

m $\overline{CD}$ = 1.00 inches

m $\overline{FE}$ = 0.72 inches

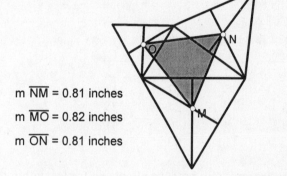

29. The figure appears to be an equilateral triangle.

m $\overline{NM}$ = 0.81 inches

m $\overline{MO}$ = 0.82 inches

m $\overline{ON}$ = 0.81 inches

31. Figure i. shows that the
     nine points lie on a circle.
     In figure ii, the Euler line
     was constructed and the
     segment joining the
     orthocenter and circum-
     center bisected. This
     point was used as the
     center of a circle with
     radius to the midpoint
     of a side. This is the same
     circle as in i.

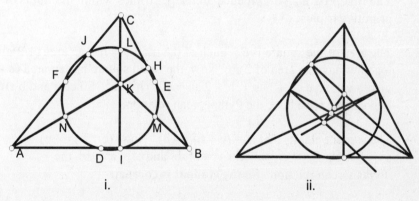

i.

ii.

33. GES suggests that the centroid is between the orthocenter and the circumcenter and divides this segment in the
     ratio 2:1. A fact that strengthens the conjecture is that the centroid is always inside a triangle while the other
     2 points may be outside a triangle. However, for an equilateral triangle all 3 points are coincident.

35. a. Responses will vary. Some students may take the approach: A trace of the program produces the
         following table of related values in which A, B, C are Pythagorean triples in which $A = M^2 - N^2$,
         $B = 2MN$, $C = M^2 + N^2$.

M	N	A	B	C
2	1	3	4	5
3	1,2	8,5	6,12	10,13
4	1,2,3	15,12,7	8,16,24	17,20,25
5	1,2,3,4	24,21,16,9	10,20,30,40	26,29,34,41

The triples are calculated by the following process: for each M and N, $C^2 = (M^2 + N^2)^2 = M^4 + 2M^2N^2 + N^4$ which can be expressed as $M^4 - 2M^2N^2 + N^4 + 4M^2N^2 = (M^2 - N^2)^2 + (2M^2N^2)^2$. So with $C^2 = (M^2 + N^2)^2$, $A^2 = M^4 - 2M^2N^2 + N^4$, and $B^2 = 4M^2N^2$ we have the Pythagorean triples $A = M^2 - N^2$, $B = 2MN$, $C = M^2 + N^2$.

b.   By increasing the upper limit of the loop of statement 10, say to FOR M = 2 to 7, additional triples can be generated.

c.   Three primitive Pythagorean triples are: (3,4,5), (5,12,13), (7,24,25).

d.   The program could be:
```
FOR N = 1 to 5
LET A = 2N + 1
LET B = 2N² + 2N
LET C = 2N² + 2N + 1
PRINT A;"""";B;"""";C
NEXT N
```
A trace of this program produces:

N	A	B	C
1	3	4	5
2	5	12	13
3	7	24	25
4	9	40	41
5	11	60	61

The first program will produce all integer triples within the limits of the loops. The second program produces primitive triples.

37.   The area of the square is c^2. Each of the triangles has an area $(1/2)ab$. So the area of the 4 triangles taken together have an area of 2 ab. Now, the small square has an area $(b - a)^2$ or $b^2 - 2ab + a^2$. So summing all the pieces we have $c^2 = 2ab + b^2 - 2ab + a^2 = b^2 + a^2$ Since a and b are the legs of a right triangle with hypotenuse c we have the Pythagorean relation.

39.   The student claims that $a^2 = (c + b)(c - b)$. Now, $(c + b)(c - b) = c^2 - cb + cb - b^2 = c^2 - b^2$. So $a^2 = c^2 - b^2$ and $c^2 = a^2 + b^2$, the Pythagorean relation. **So the student is correct.**

41.   Now, applying the Pythagorean relation we have $(b + 1)^2 = b^2 + a^2$ and $b^2 + 2b + 1 = b^2 + a^2$. So $a^2 = 2b + 1 = b + (b + 1)$, and $a = \sqrt{[b + (b + 1)]}$. Thus **the student is correct**.

a.   The second leg is $\sqrt{(7.5 + 8.5)} = \textbf{4}$.

b.   The second leg is $\sqrt{(9 + 10)} \approx \textbf{4.36}$.

c.   The second leg is $\sqrt{(40 + 41)} = \textbf{9}$.

d.   The second leg is $\sqrt{(60 + 61)} = \textbf{11}$.

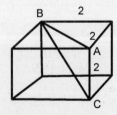

43. $AB = \sqrt{(2^2 + 2^2)} = \sqrt{8}$, so $BC = \sqrt{[2^2 + (\sqrt{8})^2]} = \sqrt{12} \approx \textbf{3.46}$.

45.   The area of the trapezoid, A, is the sum of the areas of the 3 triangles. So $A = (1/2)ab + (1/2)ab + (1/2)c^2$.
      The area of a trapezoid is also $(1/2)$altitude(base 1 + base 2). So $A = 1/2(a + b)(a + b) = 1/2(a^2 + 2ab + b^2)$.
      Thus $(1/2)ab + (1/2)ab + (1/2)c^2. = 1/2(a^2 + 2ab + b^2)$ and $a^2 + b^2 = c^2$.

SECTION 11. 3

1.   The length to width ratio of a Golden Rectangle is approximately 1.618 : 1. Because the length to width ratio
     of a 3 by 5 index card is 1.67 to 1, it is close to a Golden Rectangle. An 8 by 5 index card is closer to a
     Golden rectangle because its length to width ratio is 1.6 to 1.

3.   Responses will vary. The ratio of the lengths of segments TH and HG and the ratio of the lengths TQ and TS
     is 1.618 : 1.

5.   The star polygon {5/2} has 5 sides: AC, CE, EB, BD, and DA.

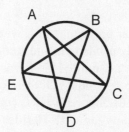

7.

   a. A segment   b. a quadrilateral   c. a triangle   d. a hexagon
       is formed.   is produced.   is formed.   results.

9.   a.   Since ABCDE is a regular pentagon, angle x measures
          $(5 - 2)(180)/5 = 108°$ and angle y, the supplement of x,
          measures 72°. Since the triangle BCF is isosceles,
          angle z measures 72°, and the angle at the point of the star
          measures $(180 - 72 - 72) = \mathbf{36°}$

     b.   The 8 points on the circle divide the circle into 8 equal arcs of 45°.
          Each point angle is an inscribed angle intercepting two of the 45° arcs.
          Since an inscribed has ½ the degree measure of the arc it
          intercepts, the point angles have measures of **45°**.

     c.   The 9 points on the circle divide the circle into 9 equal arcs of
          40°. Each point angle is an inscribed angle intercepting five
          of the 40° arcs. Since an inscribed has ½ the degree measure
          of the arc it intercepts, the point angles have measures of **100°**.

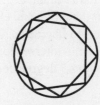

11.   ABCDEFGH is a regular octagon with interior angles of 135° All the
      triangles at the points are isosceles triangles congruent to triangle
      GHI which has a vertex angles of 15°. So the base angles of GHI are
      (180 - 15)/2 = 82.5°. Since all three angles about point H sum to
      360°, 360° = d + 82.5 + 82.5 + 135 and d, the dent angle, is equal to **60°**.

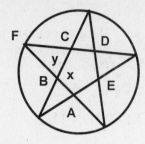

13.   Responses will vary. **No, she was not correct**.
      If the point angle is 30°, the dent angle, p, is (360°/6) + 30°, or
      90°. Since 90 degrees is the angle of a square, a square can
      fill the spaces at A, B, C, D, E, and F. However, the angle JIK
      is 140 degrees, far greater than the point angle of the
      star polygon. So the pattern cannot be extended.

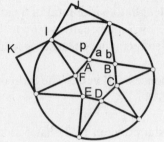

15.   To be a star polygon, {n/d}, we must have 1 < d < n-1,
      d relatively prime to n, and recognize that {n/d} is
      equivalent to {n/n-d}. So for n = 10, candidates for d
      are 2,3,4,5,6,7,and 8. Of these only 3 and 7 are relatively
      prime to 10. Since {10/3} is equivalent to {10/7}, there is
      one star polygon with 10 sides.

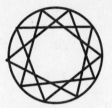

17.   Responses will vary depending upon the software used and the figures investigated. Possibilities
      include: The generalization given is: If d represents the measure of the dent angles, a represents the measure
      of the point angles, and n represents the number of point angles, then d = (360/n) + a. The figures support
      the generalization.

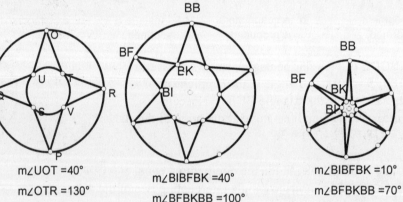

m∠UOT =40°
m∠OTR =130°

m∠BIBFBK =40°
m∠BFBKBB =100°

m∠BIBFBK =10°
m∠BFBKBB =70°

19.   Responses to this construction activity will vary. One approach is: Construct a circle with
      2 perpendicular diameters. Bisect the right angles at the center of the circle giving eight points equally
       spaced on the circle and eight radii joining these points to the center of the circle. Use the eight radii as the
      bisectors of 45 degree angles with vertexes the eight points on the circle.   The segments joining the points on
      the circle to the intersection points of consecutive angle sides are the sides of the 8 pointed star-shaped
      polygon with 45 degree point angles. Figure on the next page.

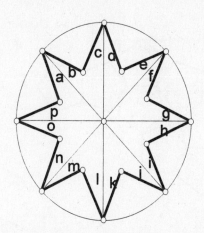

Angles a,b,...o,p are 22.5 degrees

21. Responses will vary. One possibility is: A process for constructing 6 points star polygons is to first construct a circle and the determine 6 equally spaced points on the circle. Then determine the bisectors of the angles formed by consecutive points on the circle and the center. Now construct a circle inside the first with the same center. Mark the points at which the bisectors intersect the smaller circle and connect, alternately, a point in the outside circle with a point in the inside circle. The resulting figure is a six-pointed star polygon. Because there are an infinite number of possibilities for the smaller circle, there are an infinite number of six-pointed start polygons.

    Three are:

Point Angle	Dent Angle
20	80
30	90
40	100

23. In **tessellation (a)** one may identify **squares, equilateral triangles, and regular hexagons**. The 12 pointed star shaped polygons can be considered to be caused by the placement of the first three figures. The sides of the star polygons are sides of the equilateral triangles. There are 2 types of vertices, one is surrounded by a **square, a hexagon, and 2 triangles** and can be characterized as **3,6,4,3**. The other type of vertex, at the dent of the star polygon, is a **3, star** vertex. The **dent angles** are the angles of the equilateral triangles, **60°.** The **point angles** are 60 - (360/12) = **30°**.

    In tessellation (b) the pattern can be formed from arrangements of **equilateral triangles**. The 4 pointed star shaped polygons are spaces left from the placement of the triangles. There are **2 types of vertices in** b. At one there are **4 triangles and 4 star polygons: 3,star,3,star,3,star,3,star**. At the other there are **2 triangles and a star: 3,3,star**. The **dent angles** are 2 angles from the equilateral triangles, **120°**. The **point angles** are 120 - (360/4) = **30°**.

25. Let c represent the length of the longer side of the rectangle and d represent the length of the shorter side. Since all isosceles right triangles are similar, the ratio a:b, the ratio of legs, is equal to the ratio c:d, the ratio of the hypotenuses. Since a:b is the golden ration, c;d is also the golden ration and the rectangle is a golden rectangle.

27. Since the sum of the angles about a point on one side of a line is 180°, we have $360/n + x + \alpha + x = 180$ and $360/n + \alpha + 2x = 180$. Since the sum of the angles of a triangle is 180°, we also have $\beta + 2x = 180$. So $360/n + \alpha + 2x = \beta + 2x$. Hence $360/n + \alpha = \beta$.

29. Responses will vary among groups of students. Students may investigate the orientation of the rectangles as a variable.

31.   Coloring will, of course vary.

CHAPTER 11 REVIEW EXERCISES

1.   Some Responses will vary. Possibilities include:
   a.   Pairs of non-vertical congruent angles include: 2 and 6 (corresponding), 3 and 5 (alternate interior), 1 and 7 (alternate exterior), 3 and 7 (corresponding).
   b.   Pairs of non-adjacent supplementary angles include: 4 and 5, 3 and 6, 1 and 8, 2 and 7.
   c.   Pairs of alternate interior angles are: 3 and 5, 4 and 6.
   d.   Pairs of alternate exterior angles are 2 and 8, 1 and 7.
   e.   Pairs of corresponding angles are 2 and 6, 3 and 7, 1 and 5, 4 and 8.

3.   Since the sum of the angles of any triangle is 180°, C = 180 - 54 - 78 = **48°**.

5.   Since a stop sign is a regular octagon, the angle formed by two edges is an interior angle of the octagon. The sum of the interior angles, (8 - 2)180° divided by 8 is **135°**.

7.   Responses will vary. Possibilities include:
   a.   The incenter is located at the intersection of the interior angle bisectors. It is the center of that circle that is inscribed in a triangle.
   b.   The circumcenter is located at the intersection of the perpendicular bisectors of the sides of a triangle. It is the center of that circle that will circumscribe the triangle.
   c.   The orthocenter is located at the intersection of the altitudes of a triangle.
   d.   The centroid is located at the intersection of the medians of a triangle. It is the center of mass, or balance point, of a triangular object of uniform thickness made from a material of uniform density. The centroid is located at a point 2/3 of the length of the median from the vertex from which the median is drawn.

9.   The Pythagorean Theorem relates the lengths of the sides of a right triangle. If the lengths of the legs are represented by a, b, and the hypotenuse by c, then $c^2 = a^2 + b^2$.

11.   Responses will vary. Possibilities include:
   a.   Opposite sides of a parallelogram are parallel and congruent; the diagonals bisect each other.
   b.   The diagonals of a rectangle are equal; opposite sides are equal.
   c.   All sides of a rhombus are congruent; the diagonals are perpendicular.

13.   Responses will vary from paperbacks to texts to coffee table type books. One possibility is **25 cm x 15.45 cm**.

15.   If d represents the measure of the dent angles and p the measure of the point angles of a star shaped polygon of n sides, then d = 360/n + p. So d = 360/6 + 45 = **105°**.

17. Since the sum of the exterior angles of a polygon is constant at 360° no matter the number of sides and since there is an exterior angle for each side, as the number of sides increases the measure of each exterior angle of a regular polygon decreases.

19. Assume that there are n equally spaced points on the circle. So the circle is divided into n equal arcs each each of measure (360/n)°. Each point angle is an inscribed angle intercepting an arc equal to (n - 2d) of the equal arcs. Since an inscribed angle has a measure (1/2) of the arc it intercepts, the point angle measures (1/2)(n - 2d)(360/n|). This is equivalent to (N - 2d)(180/n). So, **the generalization is true for a regular star polygon**.

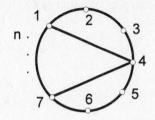

21. Let L represent the length of the ladder. Twice applying the Pythagorean theorem, we have $L^2 = d^2 + 24^2$ and $L^2 = (d/2)^2 + (24.75)^2$. So $L^2 = (L^2 - 24^2)/4 + (24.75)^2$. L ≈ **25 ft**.

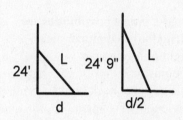

23. Responses will vary. Students should address the methods of dissection, transformations, and measurement and computation.

SECTION 12.1

1. a. Responses will vary. Representative measurements are: The width of a paperback book is about 3 1/4 paperclips and 1 1/5 index fingers.
    b. The length of a sheet of paper is about 8 3/4 paperclips or about 3 1/4 index fingers.

3. a. **grams**
    b. **kilograms**
    c. **kilograms**
    d. **milligrams**
    e. **kilograms**
    f. **grams**

5. Responses will vary. Some possibilities are:
    a. 10 cm: the length of a computer disk.
    b. 3 m: the height of a ceiling.
    c. 10 g: 2 or 3 coins.
    d. 1 lb: a couple of paper back books.
    e. 3 inches: the length of a finger.
    f. 6 yd: the length of a car.
    g. 5 kg: a median turkey.
    h. 500 ml: a really good sized glass of beer.

7. Responses will vary. Possibilities include:
    a. 16 cm   b. 5 m   c. 250 ml   d. 4 kg   e. 100 g

9. Since C = 5/9(F - 32), C = 5/9(98.6 - 32) = 5/9(66.6) = **37° C**.

11. By tracing the triangle and tessellating the parallelogram, the area is **16 units**.

13. There are various ways of dissecting the figure.
     One possibility is: Rectangle AFGK has an area
     2 x 5 = 10 units. Triangles FEL, LDC, and IJK
     each have areas of ½ unit for a total of 3/2 unit.
     Triangle ACB has half the area of rectangle
     ACBM (6 units), 3 units. Finally, triangle HIJ
     has an area half of rectangle HIJO (2 units), 1 unit.
     So the total is 10 + 3/2 + 3 + 1 = **15 ½ units**.

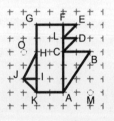

15. Estimates will vary. One possibility is: The figure is roughly square, say 30 mm on a side, with a square roughly 15 mm by 15 mm cut out. So an estimate is (30 mm)(30 mm) - (15 mm)(15 mm) , about 700 mm².

17. Since the area of a 2 in by 2 in square is 4 times the area of a 1 in by 1 in square, the measure of **area using the larger unit would be 4 times less (1/4 as great) than that using the smaller unit.**

19. Since 180 Fahrenheit degrees (the number of degrees between boiling and freezing water) correspond to 100 Celsius degrees (again, the number of degrees between boiling and freezing water), 10 Celsius degrees correspond to **18 Fahrenheit degrees**.

21. $6.20 /kg = $6.20/1000 g = $0.0062/g. Now: ($10)/($0.0062/g) = **1612.9 g** to the nearest tenth of a gram.

23. (10 g /sheet)(500 sheet/ ream) = 5000 g/ream = 5000 g/ream (1 kg/1000 g) = **5 kg /ream**.

25. Responses will vary. A possibility is: 40 km is about 24 miles or 1 km is about 0.6 miles. So to obtain a distance in miles, knowing the measure in km, multiply the measure by 0.6. Conversely, knowing a measure in miles to obtain a rough distance in km, multiply by 2. If a better estimate is required, after multiplying the number of miles by 2, subtract one third the number of miles. For example: 200 miles is about 400 km. The better estimate is 400 km - 1/3(200)km or about 330 km.

27. Responses will vary. The two primary arguments are: most of the rest of the world uses metric measures and because of the global interactions in manufacturing it is necessary to have a global standard. On the other hand, a massive reeducation effort is required to change. It has been done in other countries, South Africa is an example.

SECTION 12.2

1. To find the area of the rectangle 12 cm x 40 mm one might first change the measures to the same units, either 12 cm x 4 cm or 120 mm x 40 mm.

3. a. Perimeter = 4(6 in) = **24 in**. Area = (6 in)(6 in) = **36 in^2**.
   b. Perimeter = 2(6 m) + 2(4 m) = **20 m**. Area = (6 m)(4 m) = **24 m^2**.
   c. Perimeter = 2(2 m) + 2(12 cm)(0.01 m/cm) = **4.24 m**. Area = (2 m) (12 cm)(0.01 m/cm) = **0.24 m^2**.

5. a. Area = (6 in)(6 in) + (1/2)(6 in)(6 in) = **54 in^2**.
   b. Area = (1/2)(4 ft)(15 ft + 7 ft) = **44 ft^2**.
   c. Area = (1/2)(5 m)(10 m + 13 m) = **57.5 m^2**.
   d. Area = (1/2)(5 mm)((7 mm + 2 mm) = **22.5 mm^2**.

7. a. Circumference = 10 mm(3.14) = **31.4 mm**. Area = 3.14[(1/2)(10 mm)]^2 = **78.5 sq mm**.
   b. Circumference = 2(4 in)(3.14) = **25.12 in**. Area = 3.14(4 in)^2 = **50.24 in^2**.

9. Since perimeters of similar figures are directly proportional to lengths of corresponding sides, P/20 = 5/4. So P = (5/4)20 = **25**.

11. The number of bags, N, is: N = (90 ft)(60 ft)/(200 sq ft /bag) = **27 bags**.

13. The figures may be dissected in a variety of ways. Possible methods are:

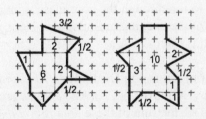

      a. Area = 15 1/2.   b. Area = 19 1/2.
         Pick's Theorem gives   Pick's Theorem gives:
         A = b/2 + i -1 =   A = b/2 + i - 1 =
         15/2 + 9 - 1 = **15 1/2**.   17/2 + 12 - 1 = **19 1/2**.

15. The largest area is **36** and the smallest is **1/2**. Because the smallest values for b and i in Pick's Theorem are 3 and 0, the smallest area is 3/2 - 0 -1 = 1/2. The largest area is the entire geoboard, 6 x 6.

17. a.   Since the legs of a 45/45/90 triangle are equal, the area is (1/2)(8 yd)(8 yd) = **32 sq yd**.
    b.   The area of an equilateral triangle is $(s^2/4)\sqrt{3}$. So the area is [(12 cm)(12 cm)/4](1.732) ≈ **62.35 sq cm**.
    c.   The base of the triangle is 7.5 m and the height 4 m. So the area is (1/2)(4 m)(7.5 m) = **15 m^2**.
    d.   Since the triangle is isosceles, the base angles are equal. But the non-base angle is 60 degrees. So the sum of the equal angles is 180 - 60 = 120 degrees. So the base angles are also 60 degrees and the triangle is equilateral. So the area is $(s^2/4)\sqrt{3}$. Thus A = [(10 mm)(10 mm)/4](1.732) ≈ **43.3 sq mm**.

19. a.   The area is (45/360)(3.14)(15 mm)^2 = **88.3 sq mm**.
    b.   The area is (150/360)(3.14)(10 cm)^2 = **130.8 sq cm**.

21. The area of a trapezoid is given by $(1/2)a(b_1 + b_2)$ or $a[(b_1 + b_2)/2]$. Now: in a rectangle $b_1 = b_2$ and in a triangle $b_2 = 0$. So the formula reduces to area = ab for a rectangle (area = altitude time base) and to (1/2)ab for a triangle. The rectangle and triangles may be considered special case trapezoids: the rectangle a trapezoid with equal bases, the triangle a trapezoid with one base 0.

23. Since the ratio of areas is the square of the ratio of perimeters of similar figures and since the ratio of corresponding sides of similar figures is the same as the ratio of perimeters, if the ratio of areas is 2/1, the **ratio of corresponding sides is $\sqrt{2}/1$ or about 1.41 to 1 and the ratio of perimeters is the same**.

25. Since the area of a rectangle is length times width and the area of a square is side squared, we have s^2 = (12 in)(27 in) = 324 sq in. So s = **18 in**.

27. Responses will vary. One possible argument is: The sides given may not be corresponding. One may be the longer side of one of the rectangles and the other the shorter side of the other rectangle.

29. Arguments will vary. A possibility is: **The rectangle becomes more elongated, or less square**. A square has the smallest perimeter for a given area. Suppose the area is 64. Then the perimeter of the square with this area is 32. Now, in order to have an area of 64, the product of the length and with must be 64. Some pairs with this product are 4 and 16, 2 and 32, 1 and 64. The respective perimeters are 40, 68, and 130. As the perimeter increases with constant area the rectangles becomes less square.

31. The area of the dartboard is (6 ft)(7 ft) = 42 sq ft. The area occupied by the balloons, the success area, is 63(3.14)[(1/2)(6 in)(1 ft/12 in)]^2 = 12.37 sq ft. Thus the probability of success is 12.37/42 = **0.29**.

33. Assuming that the time for the sand to run through the hour glass is inversely proportional to the area of the hole, to cut the time in half the area of the opening must double. Now, since the area of a circle is proportional to the square of the radius, we have $A/a = 2/1 = r^2/1^2$. So r = $\sqrt{2}(1)$ ≈ **1.4 mm**.

35. Suppose that EXF is a perpendicular to AB and to DC through X. Then the area of the parallelogram is (EF)(AB). Now, the area of triangle AXB is (1/2)(EX)(AB) and the area of triangle DCX is (1/2)(FX)(DC). Because AB has the same length as DC, the sum of these area is (1/2)AB(FX + EX) = 1/2(AB)(EF). This is one half the area of the parallelogram. So the shaded area is **one half** of the parallelogram.

37. The total area of the stores is: (70)(50) + (70)(50) + (1/2)(100)(70 + 100) = 15,500 sq ft. At a rental rate of $0.25/sq ft/month, the income would be (15,500 sq ft)($0.25/ sq ft/month) = **$3875 /month**.

39. The per sq yd price of the first parcel of land is $15,000/(50 x 90)sq yd = $3.33/sq yd and the per sq yd cost of the second is $55,000/(180 x 100) sq yd = $3.06/sq yd. The **180 x 100 sq yd plot** is the better buy.

41. The formula works if a = c and b =d (and if all 4 are equal) and if the angles are right angles: that is if the figures are rectangles or squares because it then reduces to A = length x width. It is possible that the Babylonian dissected areas into rectangles and squares.

43. Water is carried through the cross sectional area of the eaves. The original eve had a cross section of $(1/2)(a)(2 + 4)$ with $a = \sqrt{(3^2 - 1^2)} \approx 2.83$. So the original area is about 8.5 sq in. The new cross section is $(1/2)(a)(3 + 5)$ with $a = \sqrt{(4^2 - 1^2)} \approx 3.87$ in. Thus the new area is about 15.5 sq in. The increase in area is 15.5 - 8.5 = 7 sq in, an increase of (7/8.5)100% = 82%. Thus the percent increase in water flow is **approximately 82%**.

SECTION 12.3

1. a. $V = (4)(4)(4) = $ **64 cm³** $\qquad$ SA = 6[(4)(4)] = **96 cm²**
    b. $V = (4)(5)(6) = $ **120 ft³** $\qquad$ SA = 2[(4)(5)] + 2[(4)(6)] + 2(5)(6) = **148 ft²**
    c. $V = [(1/2)(3)(3)]6 = $ **27 mm³** $\qquad$ SA = 2[(1/2)(3)(3)] + 2[(3)(6)] + $3\sqrt{2}(6) \approx$ **70.5 mm²**
    d. $V = (5)(5)(6) = $ **150 m³** $\qquad$ SA = 2[(5)(5)] + 4[(5)(6)] = **170 m²**
    e. $V = (3)(5)(10) = $ **150 in³** $\qquad$ SA = 2[(3)(5)] + 2[(3)(10)] + 2[(5)(10)] = **190 in³**
    f. $V = [(2^2/4)\sqrt{3}]10 \approx $ **17.3 cm³** $\qquad$ SA = 2 [(2²/4)$\sqrt{3}$] + 3 [(2)(10)] ≈ **63.46 cm³**
    g. $V = 3.14(3^2)3 = $ **84.8 cm³** $\qquad$ SA = 2[3.14(3²)] + 3.14(6)3 = **113 cm³**
    h. $V = 3.14(1^2)9 = $ **28.26 cm³** $\qquad$ SA = 2 x 3.14(1²)9 + 3.14(2)9 = **62.8 cm²**
    i. $V = (1/3)(6)(6)(4) = $ **48 cm²** $\qquad$ SA = (6)(6) + 4(1/2)(6)$\sqrt{(3^2 + 4^2)} \approx$ **96 cm²**
    j. $V = (1/3)[(3^2/4)\sqrt{3}]4 \approx $ **5.2 m³** $\qquad$ SA = [(3²/4)$\sqrt{3}$] + 3(1/2)3a; a = $\sqrt{(4^2 + b^2)}$;
    $\qquad\qquad\qquad\qquad\qquad\qquad\qquad\qquad$ b = (1/3)$\sqrt{(3^2 - 1.5^2)} \approx$ 0.87; so a ≈ 4.09;
    $\qquad\qquad\qquad\qquad\qquad\qquad\qquad\qquad$ SA = 18.4 + 3.9 ≈ **22.3 m²**

    k. $V = (4/3)(3.14)3^3 = $ **113 in³** $\qquad$ SA = 4(3.14)3² = **113 in²**
    l. $V = (1/2)(4/3)(3.14)6^3 = $ **452 cm³** $\qquad$ SA = (1/2)4(3.14)(6²) + (3.14)(6²) = **339 cm²**

3. a. A = $2\pi R^2 + 2\pi RH$; a = $2\pi(R/2)^2 + 2\pi(R/2)(H/2) = (1/4)A$. So A/a = **4/1**.
    b. A = 2(LW + LD + WD); a = 2[(3/4)L(3/4)W + (3/4)L(3/4)D + (3/4)W(3/4)D] = (9/16)A.   So A/a = **16/9**.

5. $W = (3/4)(4)(3.14)(3850)^2 = $ **139,627,950 sq mi**.

7. a. Corresponding linear parts of similar cylinders are the radii, diameters, heights, and circumferences.
    b. Corresponding linear parts of similar spheres are radii, diameters, and great circles.
    c. Corresponding linear parts of similar cones are base radii, base diameters, heights, slant heights, base circumferences.
    d. Corresponding linear parts of similar pyramids are corresponding segments of the bases, heights, and corresponding parts of the faces.

9. Fred is making his tent in the shape of a pentagonal based pyramid. The formula for the surface area of a pyramid is B + (1/2)ph in which B represents the area of the base, p represents the perimeter of the base, and h represents the slant height or the altitude of the triangular faces. So Fred would have to measure the length, l, of a side of the regular pentagonal base to determine p; the distance from the center of the base to the middle of a side, a, to calculate the area of the base; and the distance from the top of the tent to the middle of a side of the base, h. If the tent were to have a dirt floor Fred would not need the measure B and thus would only have to measure l and h.

11. The volume of a sphere, V, with radius 5 cm is $(4/3)\pi(5 \text{ cm})^3$. So the ratio V = 523.3 cu cm. The volume of a cylinder, C, with radius 5 cm and height h is $\pi r^2(h)$ = 78.5 h. So if the volume 523.3 cu cm is poured into the cylinder, it will fill the cylinder to a height h = 523.3 cu cm/78.5 sq cm = **6.67 cm**.

13. If the container is cubical, its volume, V, is s^3, s the length of an edge. So 216 cu in = s^3 or s = $^3\sqrt{216}$ = **6 in**. Alternative sized containers will vary. Possibilities are: If the base were 4 in by 5 in the height would be 216 cu in/20 sq in = 10.8 in. So a container could be 4 in by 5 in by 10.8 in. Another possibility is 5 by 6 by 7.2. A third possibility is 3 by 5 by 14.4.

15. The rocks produce a volume increase of (2 cm)(30 cm x 60 cm) = **3 600 cu cm**.

17. Arguments will vary. **Tracy is correct**. The original volume, v, is (2 in)(3 in)(5 in) and suppose the order is lwh. Now, the new volume, V, is [(2)(2 in)][(2)(3 in)][(3)(5 in)]. But because multiplication is both commutative and associative, the multipliers can be associated with any of the dimensions and, in fact, can be factored and themselves multiplied to give V = 12[(2 in)(3 in)(5 in)].

19. The volume, C, of the pipe itself is $(500 \text{ cm})(3.14)(1.75 \text{ cm}/2)^2$, 1202.03 cu cm, and the volume, H, of the hole in the pipe is $(500 \text{ cm})(3.14)(1.5 \text{ cm}/2)^2$, 833.125 cu cm. The volume of the copper is the difference between these volumes, **318.9 cu cm**.

21. Let r represent the radius of the tennis balls. The can , a cylinder, also has base radius r and height 6 r. So the volume of the can, C, is $(\pi r^2)(6r) = 6\pi r^3$ and the volume of the 3 balls, B, is $(3)(4/3)\pi r^3 = 4\pi r^3$. So the percent of the can filled by the balls is (B/c)(100%) = **66 2/3%**.

23. The concrete fills a bottom slab, (9 x 5 x 2/12)cu ft = 7.5 cu ft;
2 end slabs, each (4 -2/12)(5)(2/12) cu ft = 3.19 cu ft,
a total 6.39 cu ft; and 2 side slabs, each (9 -4/12)(4 - 2/12)(2/12) cu ft =
5.537 cu ft, total 11.07 cu ft. The total of all 5 slabs is **25.16 cu ft**.

25. A side view of the cylinder and cone is at the right.
Triangles BGE and CED are similar so 50/6 = BD/3
and BD = 25 cm. The volume of the cylinder, C, is
$(3.14)(3^2)(25)$ = 706.5 cu cm. The volume of the cone,
V, is $(1/3)(3.14)(6^2)(50)$ = 1884 cu cm.
So, (C/V)(100%) = **37.5 %**.

27. The volume of the box, B, is (6 in)((9 in)(6 in) = 324 cu in The total volume of the 6 cans, T, is
$6(3.14)(3/2)^2 6$ cu in = 254.34 cu in. The percent filled by the cans is (254.34/324)(100%) = **78.5 %**.
Now, if the volume of the box remains at 324 cu in but the dimensions are altered so that it will hold 8 cans of radius r and height h, then the box has dimensions 4r by 8r by h and $32r^2h$ = 324 cu in. The total volume of the 8 cans is $8(3.14)r^2h = 25.12 \, r^2h$. Now, r^2h = 324/32 = 10.125 and the volume of the cans is 254.34 cu in. Thus the percent of the box filled by the cans is (254.34/324) =**78.5 %**.

29. The surface area is $(8 \times 8) + 4(8 \times 1) + 2(3 \times 4) + 2(3 \times 8) + 2(2 \times 8) + (4 \times 8) - 2(3.14)(1^2) + (3.14)(2)(4) =$
251 sq cm. The volume is $(8 \times 8 \times 4) - 2(8 \times 2 \times 3) - (3.14)(1^2)(4) =$ **147 cu cm**.

31.

Cylinder	Dimensions (d x h)	Surface area	Volume
1	(4 x 3)	20π	12π
2	(8 x 3)	56π	48π
3	(4 x 6)	32π	24π

   a. Doubling the radius with the same height more than doubles the area.
   b. Doubling the radius with the same height quadruples the volume.
   c. Doubling the height with the same radius less than doubles the surface area.
   d. Doubling the height with the same radius doubles the volume.

33. Since four squares of area x^2 are cut from a sheet with an area (15 cm)(15 cm) = 225 sq cm, the area remaining to make the box is $225 - 4x^2$. This will be minimum for the largest permissible x, **x = 7**. The area remaining is 225 - 4(49) = **29 sq cm**.

35. A volume twice that of a unit cube is 2 cu in. So 2 cu in = e^3, e the length of an edge. So $2 = \sqrt[3]{2} = $ **1.26 in**.

CHAPTER 12 REVIEW EXERCISES

1. Since 1 m = 100 cm, $(1m)^2 = (100 \text{ cm})^2 = 10,000 \text{ cm}^2$, **d**.

3. Since there are (3 ft/yd)(3 ft/yd) = 9 sq ft/ sq yd, there are 2700sq ft/ 9 sq ft/ sq yd = **300 sq yd**. **b**.

5. The area of the triangle may be calculated as (1/2)(16 in)(12 in) or as (1/2)(20 in)(BD). So we have: (1/2)(16 in.)(12 in.) = (1/2)(20 in.)(BD); BD = (12)(16)/(20) = **9.6 in., b**.

7. Suppose the length of CD is x and the altitude of the trapezoid is a. Then the area of the trapezoid is (1/2)(x + 2x)a = (3/2)xa. The area of triangle CDE is (1/2)xa. So the ratio of the trapezoid area to the triangle area is [(3/2)xa]/[(1/2)xa] = (3/2)/(1/2) is **3/1, a**.

9. The ratio of the areas of similar figures is the square of the ratio of corresponding lengths. So the area ratio is (4/1)(4/1) = **16/1, c**.

11. The volume of the cylinder is 6B, B the base area of the cylinder. The volume of the cone is (1/3)Bh, h the height of the cone. Since the volumes are equal, 6B = (1/3)Bh, and h = **18 ft**.

13. a. SA = $2(6^2/4)\sqrt{3}$ sq cm + 3(6)(10) sq cm ≈ **211 sq cm**.
    b. V = $[(6^2/4)\sqrt{3}]10$ ≈ **156 cu cm**.

15. The original area is 800 sq ft and the increased area is 924 sq ft, an increase of 124 sq ft. Thus the percent increase is (124/800)(100%) = **15.5 %**.

17. Because ECD is similar to ACB and the ratio of corresponding lengths is 1/2, the area ratio is 1 to 4. So the area of the trapezoid is 3/4 the area of ACB or 3 times the area of ECB. Thus the ratio of the areas ECD to AEDB is **3/1**.

19. The area can be dissected into an isosceles right triangle with legs 70 yds and area 2450 sq yd, a rectangle 150 yd by 30 yd with area 4500 sq yd, and a rectangle 80 yd by 70 yd with area 5600 sq yd. So the total area is 12,550 sq yd or 112,950 sq ft or 2.6 acre. The area is closer to 3 acres than to 2 acres but is about 13% shy of the 3 acre claim.

21.   The volume of the pool is (25 m)(15 m)(1.5 m) = 562.5 cu m. Since there are 1000 l/ cu m, the volume is 562,500 l. So the time to fill the pool is 562,500 l/ 20 l/min = 28,125 min or **469 hr or 19.5 days.**

23.   The ratio of the areas of similar figures is the square of the ratio of corresponding lengths. So the area ratio is the square of 27/20, $(1.35)^2$ = **1.82/1**

25.   A general solution to this problem is: Suppose that the circumference of the earth is C. Then the diameter, d, is C/π. Now, if the circumference is increased by 1 yard, then the diameter, D, is $(C + 1)/\pi = C/\pi + 1$ yd$/\pi$ = d + 11.5 in. So things about a foot high could crawl under the rope. These might include an ant and a small dog. A large dog, pig, and cow are doubtful.

27.   The house plan will vary among students.

SECTION 13.1

1. A quantity is a constant if its value does not change and a variable if it assumes different values. So:
    a. Because the path of the earth is elliptical, not circular, the distance from the earth to the sun is a **variable**.
    b. The number of moons of the earth, 1, is a **constant**.
    c. Because the number of days in a year has 2 values, 365 or 366 in leap year, it is a **variable**.
    d. Because the total cost of tickets to a movie changes with the number of tickets and with the prices of each ticket, it is a **variable**.
    e. The time for a ball to roll down a ramp is a **variable** because it depends upon the beginning position of the ball on the ramp.
    f. Although different civilizations have had different numbers of months in a year, we consider the number of months in a year to be **constant**, 12.

3. a. The variables are the sales in thousands of dollars, s, and the total earnings, T.
    b. The salesman receives a salary of $5000 and a commission of 0.01% on sales. The commission of 0.01% on dollar sales is the same as a commission of 0.0001 on dollar sales or a commission of 0.1 on sales in multiples of thousands. So, for s in thousands of dollars, **T is given by 5000 + 0.1s**.
    c. One million dollars is 1000 thousands of dollars. So earnings on sales of $1M is 5000+0.1(1000)=**$5100**.
    d. The formuli are: **B2: 0.1*A2+5000, B3: 0.1*A3+5000, B4: 0.1*A4+5000, B5: 0.1*A5+5000, B6: 0.1*A6+5000, B7: 0.1*A7+5000**.
    e. **B22: 0.1*A22+5000**.

5. The length, L, of walkway yet to be paved **x - 20** where x represents the total length of the walkway.

7. a. Let x represent the price of the items. in dollars. Then the cost is **(x + 0.08x + 2.75) or (1.08 x + 2.75)**.
    b. Let y represent the total cost. Then **y = 1.08x + 2.75**.
    c. y = 1.08(125) + 2.75 = **$137.75**.

9. A linear function is a function in which the independent variable is to the 1st power. A quadratic function has the independent variable to the 2nd power. So:
    a. y = -34 + 7x is **linear**.
    b. Because the independent variable is to the 2nd power, the function is **quadratic**.
    c. Because $y = 1/x^2$ is equivalent to $y = x^{-2}$, the function is **neither** linear nor quadratic.
    d. Because the independent variable is neither to the 1st or 2nd power, the function is **neither** linear nor quadratic.
    e. Since y = 2x + 23 - 14x is equivalent to y = -12x + 23, with x to the 1st power, the function is **linear**.
    f. $x^2 + y = 0$ is equivalent to $y = -x^2$. So the function is **quadratic**.

11. Responses will vary. Possibilities include: The perimeter of a rectangle with length l and width w is 2l + 2w or 2(l + w). So 12x + 20 = 2(l + w). Thus l + w = 6x + 10. One possibility is that **l = 6x and w = 10**. One can substitute any number for the length or the width and determine the corresponding width or length. For example, suppose that the length is 12. Then 12 + w = 6x + 10. Thus for **length = 12, width = (6x - 2); length = 5x, width = (x + 10); width = (2x - 2), length 4x + 12; width = x/2, length = (5 1/2)x + 10.**

13. Responses will vary. One possibility is: Driving at a constant speed on the interstates, the distance one travels is a function of the time that one drives. Distance is the dependent variable because distance depends upon the time spent driving.

15. A relationship is linear if equal increments in one variable are accompanied by equal increments in the other variable or if the increments in one variable are proportional to the increments in the other variable. So:
   a. As x has equal increments of 1, from 1 to 2 to 3 and so on, the increments of y are from -8 to -16, an increase of -8; from -16 to -24, an increase of -8. So the relationship is **linear** and **y = -8x**.
   b. The extended ratio of increments in x is: 1:3:3:2:1. The corresponding ratio for y is: 1:3:3:2:1. Since these extended ratios are proportional the relationship is **linear** and **y = x + 0.5**.
   c. Since for each increase of 3 for the x variable there is an increase of 3 for the y variable, the relationship is **linear** and **y = x - 2**.
   d. Since the increments of y are not equal as x increase by 5, the relationship is **nonlinear**.

17. **No**, not every equation is a function. If x is the independent variable, then for each value of x there can be only one value for the dependent variable, y. consider the equation $y = 2\sqrt{x}$. If x is 4, then because the square root of 4 is either 2 or -2, y can be 4 or -4. Thus the equation is not a function. Note that this is different from the equation $y = 2x^2$. If x = 2, then y = 4. If x = -2, then y is also 4. But for *each* value of x there is *only one* value of y.

19. Responses will vary. A possibility is: Each of the end tables, of which there must be 2, will seat 3 persons. Each of the remaining tables will seat 2 persons. So if T represents the total number of persons to be seated and t represents the number of non-end tables, we have T = 6 + 2 t. So if T = 50, t = (50-6)/2 = 22 non-end tables. So the number of tables required is 2 end tables and 22 non-end tables, **24** tables. If there are n persons to be seated, then the number of non-end tables is (n-6)/2 and the total number of tables is (n-6)/2 + 2 = **(n/2) - 1**. A fraction of a table should be considered as a full table. So to seat 25 persons, for example, 12 tables are required.

21. Three ways of representing a function are: graphs, equations, and tables.

SECTION 13.2

1.

x	0	-3	9	3
$8x^2$	0	72	648	72

   The table shows that **-3 and 3** are solutions to $8x^2 = 72$.

3. Responses vary. A possibility is: One is free to select any value for x or y and solve the equation for the other variable. So:
   a. For $x^2 + 3x = y$, let x = 0, 1, 2, 3, 4 and y = 0, 4, 10, 18, 28.
   b. Again, let x = 0, 1, 2, 3, 4. Y = 20, 20 1/3, 20 2/3, 21, 21 1/3.

5. a. 6x - 25 = 35; 6x - 25 + 25 = 35 + 25; 6x = 60; 6x/6 = 60/6; x = **10**. 6(10) - 25 = 60 - 25 = 35.
   b. 3x/4 + 6 = -12; 3x/4 + 6 - 6 = -12 - 6; 3x/4 = -18; (3x/4)(4/3) = -18(4/3); = **x = -24**. 3(-24)/4 + 6 = -18 + 6 = -12.
   c. 2.5x + 32 + 1.5 x = 20; 4x + 32 = 20; 4x + 32 - 32 = 20 - 32; 4x = -12; 4x/4 = -12/4. **x = -3**. 2.5 (-3) + 32 + 1.5(-3) = -7.5 + 32 - 4.5 = -12 + 32 = 20.
   d. 3x + 12 = -7x -28. 3x + 7x = -28 -12; 10x = -40. 10x/10 = -40/10; x = **-4**. 3(-4) + 12 = 0 and -7(-4) + 28 = 0
   e. $395 = $15x + $12.50; 395 - 12.50 = 15x + 12.50 - 12.50; 382.50 = 15x; 382.50/15 = 15x/15; **25.50** = x. 15(25.50) + 12.50 = 395.
   f. 78 = 5x/6 + 18; 78(6) = (5x/6)6 + 18(6); 468 = 5x + 108; 468 - 108 = 5x + 108 - 108; 360 = 5x; 360/5 = 5x/5; **72** = x. 5(72)/6 + 18 = 60 + 18 = 78.

7. The solutions to the quadratic equations in 1 variable are the values of x at which the y values are 0. These are the intersection points of the graphs with the x-axis.
    a. $x = 3, -4$. $(3)(3) + 3 - 12 = 0$; $(-4)(-4) -4 -12 = 0$.
    b. $x = 4.5$. $(4.5)(4.5) -9(4.5) + 20.25 = 0$.
    c. Because the graph does not intersect the x-axis, there are no solutions.
    d. The graph intersects the x-axis at approximately **x = 2.4 and x = -0.9**.

9. a. The sequence **83, +, 17, =, ÷, 4,** = results in **25**.
    b. The sequence **6, x, 24, +, 13,** = results in **157**.
    c. The sequence **32, +, 15, x, 3, ÷, 2** =results in **70.5**.

11. a. Because there is only one point of intersection of the graph with the x-axis, at $x = 1$, there is but **one** solution.
    b. Because there are 2 points of intersection, -1 and 7, there are **2** solutions.

13. Maurice took the equation $8 = -4x + 28$ and separated it into two equations: $y = 8$ and $y = -4x+28$. There is a set of (x,y) values that satisfy the first equation. Similarly, there is a set of (x,y) values that satisfy the equation $y = -4x + 28$. These sets of values are the points on the respective graphs. The point of intersection of the graphs has coordinates that make both equations true. The graphs intersect at (5,8). So, when $y = 8$, $x = 5$ and $8 = -4(5) + 28$. Therefore, the solution to the original equation is $x = 5$.

15. Responses will vary. Possibilities include: A quadratic equation has 1 solution if the discriminant, $b^2 - 4ac$, is 0. Suppose that $b = 3$, $a = 1$, $c = 9/4$ giving an equation $x^2 + 3x + 9/4 = 0$ with one solution, -3/2. A quadratic has 2 solutions if the discriminant is positive. Suppose $b = 3$, $a = 1$, $c = 2$ giving the equation $x^2 + 3x + 2 = 0$ with the 2 solutions -1, -2.

17. Since area is the product of length and width and since the length is to be twice the width, we have $288 = w(2w)$. So $288 = 2w^2$; $w^2 = 144$; $w = 12$. So the **width is 12 ft and the length is 24 ft**.

19. Without the chute we have $-1200 = -9.8 t^2$. So it takes 11.07 sec to free-fall 1200 m. The last 5 seconds must be reserved to deploy the chute. So the sky-diver can free fall for about 6 seconds.

21.

	2x	3	
2x	$4x^2$	6x	2x
3	6x	9	3
	2x	3	

The area of the square 2x+3 by 2x + 3
is: $4x^2 + 2(6x) + 9 = 4x^2 + 12x + 9$.

23. The solutions of a quadratic equation in one variable are often called zeros because, when solving the equation graphically, the solutions are the values of x for which the y value is zero. Also, when factoring a quadratic in one variable we obtain the solutions by setting the factors separately equal to zero.

SECTION 13.3

1.

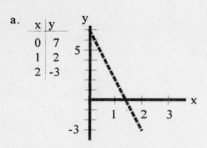
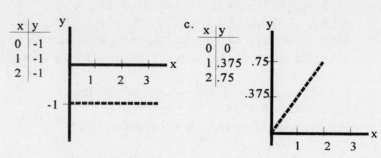

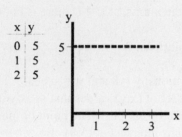
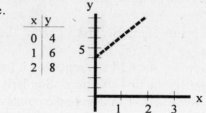

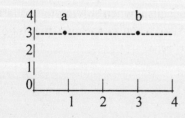

3. a. Because the slope is the coefficient of the x term, the slope is **-1**. When the equation is solved for y, the y- intercept" is the constant term: **3**.
    b. The slope is ½ and the y-intercept is **0**.
    c. Solving for y we get: y = -x + 1/2. The slope is **-1** and the y-intercept is **1/2**.
    d. Solving for y: y = (-1/4)x + + 3. so the slope is **-1/4** and the y-intercept is **3**.
    e. The slope is **16** and the y-intercept is **-120**.
    f. The data shows that when x = 0 y = 6. So the **y-intercept is 6**. As x changes by 1 unit y changes by 4 units, so the **slope is 4**.
    g. The data shows that as x changes by 5 units y changes by 40 units. So the **slope is 40/5 = 8**. Since as x increases by 5 units y increases by 40 units, if x decreases by 5 units then y decreases by 40 units. So when x goes from 5 to 0 y goes from -80 to -120. Thus the **y-intercept is -120**.

5. Responses will vary. Two lines are perpendicular if the product of their slopes is -1 or if one is vertical and the other horizontal.
    a. A line perpendicular to y = 3x + 8 has a slope of -1/3. The equation y = (-1/3)x + 1 will produce a graph that is perpendicular to the graph of y = 3x + 8.
    b. Since the slope of the graph of 2x + y = -9 is -2, the equation y = (1/2)x - 3 will produce a perpendicular line.
    c. Since y = 12 is horizontal, x = 6 will give a perpendicular line.
    d. Since the slope of y = -5(3x+ 1) is -15, y = (1/15)x will give a perpendicular graph.

7.

```
4|    a              b
3|------•--------------•-------
2|
1|
0|____|____|____|____|
     1    2    3    4
```

The slope of a graph relates the changes in y values to the changes in x values. The points a and b on the graph have the same y values. So the y values do not change, or have a change of 0, as as the x values change. Thus the slope is 0.

9. A rate is a value per unit of something. In the equation $y = 12x + 5$ the 12 is a unit cost, the cost per ticket. So **it can be thought of as a rate**.

11. If (x_1, y_1) and (x_2, y_2) are points on a line, then the slope, m, is $(y_2 - y_1)/(x_2 - x_1)$ We have (1,2) a point on the line. Let (x,y) be any other point on the line. Since the slope is known to be 1/3, we have: $1/3 = (y-2)/(x-1)$; $x - 1 = 3(y - 2)$; $x - 1 = 3y - 6$. $3y = x + 5$; **$y = (1/3)x + 5/3$**.

13. Suppose the points are (x_2, y_1) and (x_2, y_2). Correctly the slope is either $(y_2 - y_1)/(x_2 - x_1)$ or $(y_1 - y_2)/(x_1 - x_2)$. If the slope is incorrectly calculated as $(y_2 - y_1)/(x_1 - x_2)$ the result will be the opposite of the correct value. This is because $-(x_2 - x_1) = (x_1 - x_2)$.

15. To determine the slope of the line representing the relationship, we calculate $(1.40 - 0.75)/(2 - 1) = .65$. We can now find the equation of the line: $y - 0.75 = 0.65(x - 1)$; $y = 0.65x + .10$. When $y = 3.35$, we have $3.35 = 0.65x + 0.10$. So $x = 5$. Therefore, there would be **5 liters** in the container.

17. Responses will vary among students.

SECTION 13.4

1. AD: A(-6,7), D(6,7).   M(x,y): $x = (1/2)(-6 + 6) = 0$, $y = (1/2)(7 + 7) = 7$.   **M(0,7)**
    BE: B(-8,4), E(-8,-4).   M(x,y): $x = (1/2)(-8 + -8) = -8$, $y = (1/2)(4 + -4) = 0$.   **M(-8,0)**
    GH: C(-3,0), H(6,0).   M(x,y): $x = (1/2)(-3 + 6) = 1.5$, $y = (1/2)(0 + 0) = 0$.   **M(1.5,0)**
    FK: F(0, -4), K(6,-10).   M(x,y): $x = (1/2)(0 + 6) = 3$, $y = (1/2)(-4 + -10) = -7$. **M(3,-7)**

3. If (x_1, y_1) and (x_2, y_2) are the endpoints of a segment and M is the midpoint with coordinates (m,n), then $m = (x_1 + x_2)/2$ and $n = (y_1 + y_2)/2$. So:
    a. $3 = (6 + x_2)/2$; $5 = (4 + y_2)/2$.   Thus $(x_2, y_2) = $ **(0,6)**.
    b. $-2.5 = (-5 + x_2)/2$; $-1 = (3 + y_2)/2$. Thus $(x_2, y_2) = $ **(0,-5)**.
    c. $4 = (0 + x_2)/2$; $-3 = (0 + y_2)/2$.   Thus $(x_2, y_2) = $ **(8,-6)**.
    d. $0 = (7 + x_2)/2$; $0 = (7 + y_2)/2$.   Thus $(x_2, y_2) = $ **(-7,-7)**.

5. Since the distance between 2 points is the length of the segment joining them, if the coordinates of the points are (x_1, y_1) and (x_2, y_2) , then the distance is $\sqrt{[(x_2 - x_1)^2 + (y_2 - y_1)^2]}$. So:
    a. $d = \sqrt{[(0 - 0)^2 + (6 - {}^-5)^2]} = \sqrt{(11)^2} = $ **11**.
    b. $d = \sqrt{[(3 - 8)^2 + (5 - 2)^2]} = \sqrt{(34)} \approx $ **5.83**.
    c. $d = \sqrt{[(0 - 12)^2 + (0 - {}^-4)^2]} = \sqrt{(160)} \approx $ **12.64**.
    d. $d = \sqrt{[(-3 - {}^-4)^2 + (-7 - 15)^2]} = \sqrt{(485)} \approx $ **22.02**.

7. The equation of a line with slope m and y intercept b is $y = mx + b$, so:
    a. **$y = 4x - 2$**.
    b. **$y = (1/2)x + 3/4$**.
    c. **$y = -x$**.
    d. **$y = 5$**.

9. If two points of a line have coordinates (x_1, y_1) and (x_2, y_2), then the slope, m, is $(y_2 - y_1)/(x_2 - x_1)$. If the line crosses the y axis at (0,b), then b is the y-intercept and the equation of the line is $y = mx + b$. So:
    a. $m = 2/5$, $b = 3$ and **$y = (2/5) x + 3$**.
    b. $m = -6/8$, $b = 6$ and $y = $ **$(-3/4) x + 6$**.
    c. $m = 20/2$, $b = 0$ and $y = $ **10 x**.

11. The equation of a circle with center located at (h,k) ans with radius of length r is $(x - h)^2 + (y - k)^2 = r^2$. So:
   a. $(x - 0)^2 + (y - 0)^2 = 6^2$. $y^2 + x^2 = 36$.
   b. $(x - 1)^2 + (y - 2)^2 = 1/4$.
   c. $(x + 3)^2 + (y - 4)^2 = 4$.
   d. $(x + 2)^2 + (y + 1)^2 = 25$.

13. Responses will vary. But since parallel line have the same slope, all answers should be of the form $y = -2x + b$, b not equal to -3. So a possibility is $y = -2x + 2$.

15. The product of the slopes of perpendicular lines is -1. The slope of the graph of $-x/2 + 7$ is $-(1/2)$. Since the product of $-(1/2)$ and 2 is -1, the slope of lines perpendicular to the given line is 2 and they have equations of the form $y = 2x + b$. One such line has the equation $y = 2x + 5$.

17. Responses will vary. The equations of graphs of circles centered at the origin have the form $x^2 + y^2 = r^2$. Because the squares of real numbers are positive, the sum $x^2 + y^2$ is positive. Thus the right side of the equation must also be positive and thus cannot be -49.

19. The vertex of the shaded triangle is at (4.5,2) and the endpoints of the base are at (0,0) and (9,0). Thus the two sides have lengths $\sqrt{[(2 - 0)^2 + (4.5 - 0)^2]}$ and $\sqrt{[(2 - 0)^2 + (9 - 4.5)^2]}$. Since they are equal, the triangle is **isosceles**.

21. The midpoint of the segment has coordinates $[(4-3)/2, (3 + 1)/2] = (1/2, 2)$ and the segment has slope $(3 - 1)/(-3 - 4) = -(2/7)$. Thus the perpendicular bisector has slope 7/2 and passes through (1/2, 2). Using the point/slope form, we have $(y - 2)/(x - 1/2) = 7/2$, **$y = (7/2)x + 1/4$**.

23. Since the equation of a circle has the form $x^2 + y^2 = r^2$, the smaller circle has radius 4 and area 50.24 sq. Units and the larger circle has radius 9 and area 254.34 sq units. Thus the area between circles is the difference between the two areas, **204.1 sq units**.

25. The coordinates of four points can easily be read from the graph: **(0,4), (3,1), (3, 7), and (6, 4)**. Since the equation of the circle is $(x - 3)^2 + (y - 4)^2 = (9)^2$, the coordinates of a fifth point may be determined by substituting some x value between 0 and 6 into the equation and solving for y. For example, for x = 1, $y = 4 \pm\sqrt{5}$. So a fifth point is **(1, 6.236)**.

27.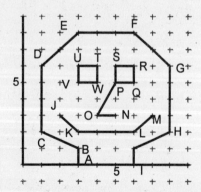

The equations are:

AB: $x = 3$

BC: $y = -1/2\ x + 2\ 1/2$

CD: $x = 1$

DE: $y = x + 5$

EF: $y = 8$

FG: $y = -x + 14$

GH: $x = 8$

HZ: $y = 1/2\ x - 2$

ZI: $x = 6$

JK: $y = -x + 5$

KL: $y = 2$

LM: $y = x - 4$

NO: $y = 3$

OP: $y = 2x - 5$

PQ: $y = 5$

QR: $x = 6$

RS: $y = 6$

SP: $x = 5$

UV: $x = 3$

VW: $y = 5$

WT: $x = 4$

TU: $y = 6$

The intersections are:

A: (3,0)

B: (3,1)

C: (1,2)

D: (1,6)

E: (3,8)

F: (6,8)

G: (8,6)

H: (8,2)

I: (6,0)

J: (2,3)

K: (3,2)

L: (6,2)

M: (7,3)

N: (5,3)

O: (4,3)

P: (5,5)

Q: (6,5)

R: (6,6)

S: (5,6)

T: (4,6)

U: (3,6)

V: (3,5)

W: (4,5)

Z: (6,1)

29. Responses will vary. Possibilities include:

 a. (3,4) --> (3+2,4+5) --> (5,9) by translating 2 over and 5 up.

 b. (3,4) --> (-3,-4) by rotating 180 degrees about the origin.

 c. (3,4) --> (-4,3) by rotating 90 degrees about the origin.

 d. (3,4) --> (4,3) by reflecting over the line $y = x$.

 e. (3,4) --> (3, -4) by reflecting over the x axis.

 f. (3,4) --> (-3,4) by reflecting over the y axis.

31. Responses will vary. The use of the slope/intercept, point/slope, intercept/intercept, or general 2-point form of the equation of a straight line depends upon the information at hand.

CHAPTER 13 REVIEW EXERCISES

1. a. The number of hours of sunlight in a day is a variable: relatively few in winter, more in summer.

 b. The number of hours in a day is constant: 24.

3. a. Let x = the number of hours worked. Then the total cost is $35 + \$9.50x$.

 b. Let C represent the total cost. Then $C = 35 + 9.50x$.

 c. $C = 35 + 9.50(8) =$ **$111**.

5. a. $4x - 18 = 65$; $4x - 18 + 18 = 65 + 18$; $4x = 83$ $(4x)/4 = 83/4$; $x =$ **20.75**.

 b. $3x + 15 = -4x - 20$; $3x + 4x + 15 = -4x + 4x - 20$; $7x + 15 = -20$; $7x + 15 - 15 = -20 - 15$; $7x = -35$; $7x/7 = (-35)/7$; $x =$ **-5**.

7. Since the graph intersects the x-axis at $x = 3$ and at $x = -5$, the solutions to $x^2 + 2x - 15$ are **3, -5**.

9. The slope is $(20 - 11)/(18 - 3) = 9/15 =$ **3/5**.

11. Since the distance between 2 points is the length of the segment joining them, if the coordinates of the points are (x_1, y_1) and (x_2, y_2), then the distance is $\sqrt{[(x_2 - x_1)^2 + (y_2 . y_1)^2]}$. So:

 a. $d = \sqrt{[(12-4)^2 + (6-5)^2]} = \sqrt{(65)} \approx$ **8.06**.

 b. $d = \sqrt{[(0 - -5)^2 + (12 - 5)^2]} = \sqrt{(74)} \approx$ **8.60**.

13. The equation of a circle with center located at (h,k) ans with radius of length r is $(x - h)^2 + (y - k)^2 = r^2$. So: $(x - 4)^2 + (y - 3)^2 = 3^2$. **$(x-4)^2 + (y+3)^2 = 9$**.

15. Responses will vary. The line must have a different slope but the same y-intercept. For example: **y = 3x + 11**.

17. When equations are solved for y, if the independent variable is to the first power, the equation is linear. If it is to the second power, the equation is quadratic. But an equation with the independent variable neither to the first nor to the second power is not linear or quadratic. For example: $y = 2x^3 + 2x - 3$.

19. The volume of a box is l x w x h. Boxes like those shown have volumes, V, (8 -2x)(10 - 2x)x.

x	1	1.5	2	2.5	3
V	48	52.5	48	37.5	24

As x increases the volume first increases and then decreases. The volume is a maximum in the vicinity of x = 1.5.

21. Responses will vary. Since distinct parallel lines have the same slope but different y-intercepts, the equation of one line parallel to y = -3x + 9 is y = -3x + 2.

23. Since in a reflection across the x axis (x,y) --> (x, -y), (-2,1) --> **(-2, -1)**; (-5,1) --> **(-5, -1)**; (-2,3) --> **(-2, -3)**.

25. If 3 and 4 are solutions to a quadratic, then they are the 'zeros' of the equation. So (x - 3) = 0 and (x - 4) = 0. So the quadratic expression is (x - 3)(x - 4), or $x^2 - 7x + 12$ and the equation is $x^2 - 7x + 12 = 0$.

27. Responses will vary. The method depends on the information at hand. Essentially there are ways depending upon what is known. If one knows the slope and y intercept the equation can be directly written in the form y = mx + b, m being the slope and b the y intercept.   If the coordinates of two points (x_1, y_1) and (x_2,y_2) are known, then the two point form, $(y - y_1)/(x-x_1) = (y_2 - y_1)/(x_2 - x_1) =$ may be used. If the line is on a graph, coordinates may be read from the graph.